FROM THE AUTHOR:

"Both in my personal life and in my professional career as a marriage and family counselor I have come to realize that staying happily married in today's world is a complex process requiring much toil and expenditure of energy by the married partners. There must be work in order for there to be play. The negotiation and resolution of our anger and the ordinary interaction of daily living are the offices and the factories where we perform the work in our marriages. Sex is the play that is made possible by that work. To separate one from the other empties both of their fullest meaning."

About the Author

Dennis Guernsey is executive director of Family Ministries in Whittier, California. He received the B.A. from Biola College, the Th.M. from Dallas Theological Seminary, the M.A. from North Texas State, and the Ph.D. from the University of Southern California.

Dr. Guernsey, a licensed marriage and family counselor, has worked with families since 1966 when, he says, "God touched my life and called me to be a missionary to the family."

D0092495

Thoroughly Married

Dennis Guernsey

A Key-Word Book
WORD BOOKS, PUBLISHER
WACO, TEXAS

THOROUGHLY MARRIED

A KEY-WORD BOOK

First Key-Word edition, March 1977
Second Key-Word edition, June 1979

ISBN: 0-87680-807-0

Library of Congress Catalog Card Number: 75-19903

Copyright © 1975 by Word Incorporated

Printed in the United States of America

To Lucy.
    I, too, rise up and call
her blessed.

Contents

Preface 9

Acknowledgments 11

1. Becoming a Lover 13

2. Preparing Your Marriage for Lovemaking .. 26

3. Preparing Your Wife for Lovemaking 39

4. Preparing Your Husband for Lovemaking .. 53

5. Understanding Your Wife's Sexuality 73

6. Understanding Your Husband's Sexuality .. 92

7. Free to Enjoy Your Sexuality 106

8. When There Are Problems 117

Reading List 127

Preface

The writing of this book proved to be a microcosm of our marriage. In the final stages of the manuscript Lucy, my wife, agreed to type the copy that was to be sent to the publisher. I gave her my work and then sat back apprehensively waiting for the finished product.

She worked and typed late into the night. The next morning she approached with chapter one. She handed it to me hurriedly walking out of the room saying little. As I read her typed manuscript I realized that she had changed it dramatically and in some places drastically. She had not only edited the manuscript for style but also for content.

Typically, my first response was to confront her with a "How could you?" kind of attitude. My fuse was short and an argument was certain to follow. But before I lashed out in complete frustration I caught myself and decided that the story I was sharing in the book was really our story and not just mine. She had as much right to edit as I did to write.

If what I was trying to say in the text of the book had any validity at all, it had to work in the relationship between us then and there.

What followed was a rather lengthy, often heated, mostly gratifying process of negotiation during which time we both had to give and take. The results of those negotiations are before you now.

Frankly, that's what this book is all about: the ebb and flow, the give and take of Christian marriage.

Both in my personal life and in my professional career as a marriage and family counselor I have come to realize that staying happily married in today's world is a complex process requiring much toil and expenditure of energy by the married partners. There must be work in order for there to be play. The negotiation and resolution of our anger and the ordinary interaction of daily living are the offices and the factories where we perform the work in our marriages. Sex is the play that is made possible by that work. To separate one from the other empties both of their fullest meaning.

This book is an attempt to examine the essence of being married, the work and play of the relationship between husband and wife, in a practical and biblical manner. Its suggestions are rooted, hopefully, in the compatible soils of God's Word and real, day-to-day living.

As you read it, I wish you well.

DENNIS B. GUERNSEY
Yorba Linda, California,
Summer, 1975

Acknowledgments

Any author, if he is honest with himself is deeply indebted to others for their contributions to his work. I am certainly no exception. In particular I would like to thank the authors and researchers of the following books for having added immeasurably to me both personally and professionally.

William Masters and Virginia Johnson, *Human Sexual Response* and *Human Sexual Inadequacy*, Little, Brown and Co., 1965, 1970.

Helen Singer Kaplan, *The New Sex Therapy*, Brunner/Mazel, 1974.

William E. Hartman and Marilyn A. Fithian, *Treatment of Sexual Dysfunction*, Center for Marital and Sexual Studies, 1972.

Seymour Fisher, *The Female Orgasm, Psychology, Physiology, Fantasy*, Basic Books, 1973.

Also, it goes without saying that others: teachers, friends, and family, have contributed as well. I simply acknowledge my debt and hope that they—and most know who they are—will be pleased with the outcome.

1

Becoming a Lover

I remember the first time I fell in love. In my memories of early adolescence, the experience stands out as one of those signposts on the road to growing up. Looking back, I now realize that the way I "fell in love" the first time was indicative of what "falling in love" would mean to me in the future.

I had gone to visit my aunt and uncle at their home near the beach. Since I had been there before, I anticipated nothing more than the usual swimming and goofing around. But this summer was to be different. My cousin had invited someone else along for the weekend—a girl! My first response was that the whole weekend was shot. Up until that point in my life girls had always been "dumb" and "yucky." I had no reason to think she would be any different.

I remember being shy when we were introduced, but found the courage to talk to her when we were alone. To be honest, I don't remember her name, and have only a faint recollection of what she looked like. However, when I close my eyes and try to visualize what we did, I have a vague sensation of talking and walking in the sun with the warm sand under my feet. We spent nearly the entire time together. Rather than the weekend being ruined, it was the best one I had ever known. For some reason this girl was different.

But, like all summer weekends this one came to an end. We had to go home. It was my first "farewell." She had to leave early because she lived farther away than me. I can remember standing around at the depot waiting for her bus to come, feeling like my arms and legs were dead weights hanging at the corners of my body with no purpose whatever. I couldn't talk to her and felt terribly uncomfortable. Her bus came, and as she walked up the steps I can remember feeling sick inside, a kind of nauseous sensation in the pit of my stomach. Her bus pulled away and she waved. My cousin who had been an observer for the whole weekend, turned to me and asked "what's wrong with you?" "I'm sick to my stomach," I said. Something was going on inside me that I had never experienced before. His reply explained my feelings, "Aw, you're not sick, Dennis. You're just in love." He was right. I had never been in love before, and didn't know that being in love meant being attracted to a girl so much that she made me feel sick inside. What a revelation! The boy was becoming a man. I was growing up.

For years that summer experience became the test of whether or not I was really in love. In fact, my insistence on that kind of sensation kept me from saying I was "in love" through most of my adolescent years. I was a "man of honor." My friends could tell a girl that they were "in love" with her and not feel the least dishonest. But, I couldn't. My rule of thumb was rigidly held to: sexual attraction plus a nauseous sensation in the pit of my stomach equaled being "in love." I had formed a point of reference that would unconsciously guide my thinking for years to come. Later it would become a source of deep pain.

When I think about it today, such a definition of love sounds grossly adolescent. You would think that as I matured physically and emotionally that my understanding of what it meant to be "in love" would also. But, it wasn't to be.

A month before I graduated from high school I became a Christian and decided to attend a Christian college, a decision that was totally inconsistent with the secular life I had lived up until that point. I became a "new creature in Christ." "Old things were passed away and all things were becoming new." I was excited with my new life.

Because so many of my pre-Christian dating experiences had been sexually oriented, I deliberately de-sexualized my relationship with girls. For two years I refused to let myself even think of being sexually attracted to a girl, let alone falling in love. At the end of those two years everything changed. I "fell in love." I met the girl who was to become my wife. We had dated only once or twice before I knew (using the old rule of thumb) that I was really "in love." She aroused me sexually and made me feel delightfully "icky." All I had to do was see her coming down the halls or waiting for me in the school library and the feeling nearly overwhelmed me.

I must admit that I didn't "turn her on" until months later, but really, that was irrelevant. The important thing was that I was "in love." The months passed and eventually she got "sick" of me too. I proposed, she accepted, and we were engaged.

A short time into our engagement problems began to arise. We began to hurt each other's feelings, and we got into fights. One night after an especially livid battle she dramatically tore off her engagement ring, threw it at me, and stormed off supposedly never to see me again. During the days that followed I remember a vague fear stirring inside me that maybe I wasn't "in love." After all, when we fought I certainly didn't feel like I felt the first time I saw her. I wasn't nauseous. I was angry. I remember asking myself the question, "Are you really in love?" I certainly missed her, but something was changing inside of me. I pushed aside my fears. A few days later I called and apologized. I'm not too sure how I pulled it off, but she wanted to come back to me. We had passed a test and were ready to move one step deeper into our relationship. I can remember driving home after we had been reconciled and feeling the aura of being "in love" again. The glow had returned.

A few months later we were married. On our wedding day I was miserably sick to my stomach and noticeably sexually aroused with anticipation. When I saw her coming down the aisle, I can remember knowing that I was "in love" because the rule of thumb was holding true. Whatever fears had arisen in the days before we were married were stilled at that moment. You need only to look at our wedding pictures and you can tell we were "in love." I have a big dumb grin on my face, and she has a shy nervous smile. Like all newly married couples, we left the church together and later that night we "made love." A new dimension to the word—we had been "in love," and now we "made love." The sexual anticipation was complete. We were together forever, and that was all that mattered then.

In the next year I finished college, worked part-time and made plans for the future. She worked full-time, and devoted much of her creative energy to becoming a homemaker. There were good times and hard times that year. The old rule of thumb was holding, I was still "in love."

Following college I entered seminary in preparation for vocational Christian service. My heart was committed fully to God and my earnest desire was to serve him. My wife was with me 100 percent. However, clouds began to appear in our marriage.

Four years, two children, and hundreds of quarrels later, I came to a place in my marriage where, again, I began to question whether or not I was "in love." The rule of thumb worked less and less. I became strongly aware of being sexually attracted to other women, but this was unacceptable for me. Again, I swept my fears and frustrations under the rug. I buried myself in school and a job and somehow we kept it together.

My wife has since shared with me that these were very difficult years for her, too. She often felt like giving up. She was hurting, but for some reason I couldn't see or hear what she tried to tell me. Maybe I didn't really care.

Following graduation from seminary we accepted a position on the staff of a large church in Southern California. I silently hoped that our return to California and the change would somehow make our marriage better. I was naïve. Nothing really changed. Whatever love is, geography rarely makes it better, and often makes it worse.

Our first year back in California was a year marked with personal tragedy. Our oldest child, a boy, accidentally drowned in a neighbor's swimming pool. Our grief was overwhelming. Neither of us had ever suffered as we did then. No one else understood my hurt as much as my wife did, and no one else felt her pain like I did. But within a year we had retreated into the old communication patterns that had served us so poorly for years. The experience of shared grief did not rekindle the old love.

I kept waiting for something to happen—a miracle perhaps—but nothing did. Finally, I decided that I wasn't "in love" with my wife any longer. That was a bad day, a terrible time. I couldn't deny the way I felt any longer, but neither did I feel that I could tell her. I had come to the end of my marital rope. I can't express how helpless and desperately alone I felt.

In desperation, I got down on my knees and cried out to God. I wasn't dumb enough to think that it was all her. In fact, I had a deep-seated fear that the problem was really mine and not hers, but I didn't know what it was. Something *was* wrong and I needed God to let me know what the problem was.

I decided to try to understand what married love was really supposed to be. I began to read in a way that I had never read before. There was much at stake.

I believe that God brought together a mixture of inputs in answer to my prayer: the direct influence of Scripture, an unusual personal experience, and my reflections about what both of these meant.

I was working as the director of a counseling center of a large church, and had a number of clients. One was an attractive young lady who had been hospitalized a number of times for emotional illness. I had been working with her for five or six months when one evening very late I received a telephone call from her husband. They had quarreled and she was curled up on the sofa in a fetal position and was refusing to talk to him. In fact, she was completely "out of touch." What should he do, he asked. I asked the usual clinical questions, and as I did, it became clear, even over the telephone, that she had retreated into a catatonic state. It had happened before. She had been hospitalized then, perhaps she would have to be hospitalized again now. I suggested that he call an ambulance and have her transferred to the nearest psychiatric hospital. His first response was a long silence, then he began to cry. "Couldn't you help?" "Would you please try something else before I have to send her away again?" "Would you please come over to our apartment and try to talk to her?" "She seems to be asking for you." It had been a long day and I was tired. It had started with an early breakfast meeting, followed by a full day of counseling at the office, prayer meeting, an officers planning meeting. I had just crawled into bed and was yearning for a good night's rest. I really had no desire to exert the necessary emotion and effort it would take to treat a psychotic in her present state. I said that my coming over wouldn't help, probably. He asked again. I refused again. But he persisted. He was obviously scared, desperate, and down to his last hope. Even though I didn't want to I had to

19

say yes. I could feel the tension at the other end of the telephone begin to lift. I was going to come. He wouldn't be alone.

I pulled myself out of bed and got dressed hurriedly, thinking to myself, "Why can't people have these kind of situations at a more convenient hour?" "Why can't they think about my needs?" I was feeling completely unsympathetic and put-upon. But I got into the car and went anyway.

Twenty miles later, and after much difficulty finding a parking place, I found their apartment and knocked on their door. He opened the door and almost collapsed with relief. I had come and he wasn't alone. The living room was brightly lit and furnished in early newlywed. Two steps into the room and I saw my client twisted like a pretzel, lying on the sofa. Her lips were moving, but I couldn't understand what she was saying. She was really "out of touch." I sent him out of the room, told him to stay out, and to pray for me. As he raced from the room he began to pray out loud with an urgency that, I'm certain, touched God's heart. I pulled a chrome chair from the kitchen table as I sat down beside her. I spoke her name and could barely disguise my feelings of anger for having to be there. I spoke her name again and grabbed her by the arm and shook her. "For crying out loud, lets get this over with so I can go home! Don't you understand that I'm tired?" Almost imperceptibly, she turned her head as she recognized my voice. Her eyes filled with tears and her face began to twist as if in agony. Before I could prepare myself, she let out a scream and uncoiled from the sofa hitting me full force in the chest. We tumbled backwards onto the floor her arms wrapped around me, clutching and tearing in total panic. Her husband rushed out of the bedroom and cried, "What's happening?" "It's okay," I reassured him. Then she began to cry, and he began to cry, and so did I. Deep from within, the sobs poured out and she clung to me like a frightened two-year-old. "Dennis, you came and I didn't think you would." "You really care." "You really love me." "Nobody else would have come." "You really love me." What could I say? I couldn't tell them that I was there out of pure obligation, that I really didn't want to come. Instead, I gently rubbed her back and gently rocked her back and forth, sitting on the floor, leaning on the sofa. I'm not too sure how much time went by, but I do remember that I wasn't tired anymore. The excitement and emotion of it all had rinsed the weariness from by body and mind. She was back in touch again and wouldn't have to be hospitalized.

Later, over a cup of tea they both grasped my hand and thanked me for coming. I had come, and that meant that I loved her. That I really cared. Inside I cringed from the embarrassment, but had the presence of mind not to say anything. I arranged for her to come into the office later in the day and quietly left for home. The twenty miles that were so long in coming, were now short. All the way home I was thinking, "if they only knew how I really felt, they wouldn't say that I cared, that I loved them." And, then it struck me. Maybe I don't know what love is really all about myself. Earlier that week I had cried out to God for help in my marriage. I had told him that I was no longer "in love" with my wife. Maybe, just maybe, I'm confused as to the meaning and purpose of love. I tucked that thought away in my subconscious and continued the drive home.

The next day, I believe that I was miraculously led by the Spirit of God to a passage of Scripture in the Book of 1 John, chapter three, verses sixteen through eighteen:

> By this we come to know—progressively to recognize, to perceive, to understand, the [essential] love: that he laid down his [own] life for us; and we ought to lay [our] lives down for [those who are our] brothers [in him].
> But if anyone has this world's goods—resources for sustaining life—and sees his brother and fellow believer in need, yet closes his heart of compassion against him, how can the love of God live and remain in him?
> Little children, let us not love [merely] in theory or in speech but in deed and in truth—in practice and in sincerity (Amplified).

It was as if God was letting me know that my old, well worn, "rule of thumb" was really only part of what mature love is. Three facts leapt out to me from this passage.

First, love is a giving of yourself, irrespective of whether or not there are feelings attached. Sometimes they are present, sometimes they are not. The greatest act of love the world has ever known, the death of Christ for our sins, involved the participant (Jesus Christ) praying for the "cup to pass" (the garden of Gethsemene prayer), and yet going ahead with it as an act of endurance (Hebrews 12:2). If that truth was obvious to everyone else, it hadn't been to me. Love had meant the romantic feelings inside that are intermixed with sexual attraction. But Jesus Christ didn't have any romantic feelings rumbling inside his gut when he hung on the cross. Quite the contrary, his love was not dependent upon feelings. It was dependent upon his seeking the best interest of others. In the case of the Lord Jesus, that involved the cross. In the case of my client, it had involved my going to that apartment in the middle of the night, even when I didn't want to. What was important was that they needed me to come, and I came. Because I did what was best for them, what they needed, it meant that I really did love them. That truth set me free. I began to wean myself from a deeply entrenched presupposition called "romantic love." The effect upon me and my marriage is noticeable to this day.

The second fact that hit me was that *mature love seeks to practically and demonstrably meet the other person's needs (verse 17)*. I'm afraid I struck out at this point. As the only child of a single parent, I had been reared to think of myself first, last, and always. In growing up, I saw to it that my needs were met, and so did my mother. When I got married I simply transferred this same expectation into my marriage. I would see to it that my needs were met and so would my wife. But the unfortunate fact was that in the process no one was seeking to meet my wife's needs. She served me and she served the children, no one served her needs. After years of this kind of selfishness, her belief that I would seek to meet her needs had atrophied. It was "me first" and rarely was there anything left over for her. This was especially true sexually. We had grown into the habit of me going to the well and finding satisfaction for my needs, but never trying to meet hers. The more often I did, the less responsive she became. At the peak of our troubles, every time we had sex, it was preceded with an argument and consummated with her giving in. I have since come to realize that my selfishness inevitably provokes a passive reluctance in her and when it happens, often the basic problem is mine, not hers.

Finally, a third truth struck me. *Mature love relies not on good thoughts and tender words to demonstrate its reality.* Instead, it relies upon actions and sincere practice (verse 18).

I am by nature a verbal person. I have always been able to express myself well and talk myself into and out of trouble. When it came to "sounding like a lover" I've never had a problem. I can make it sound absolutely reasonable in describing why something did or did not happen; in fact I can make it sound like the best course of action. However, in married love, there comes a time when words and thoughts have to be followed up with consistent actions and deeds. It's one thing to say you love someone and another to show them that you do by your actions. Imagine where we would be if the Lord Jesus only talked about the cross, but never followed through. His words would have been starkly empty, and so were mine in terms of action. God impressed on my heart that I am a selfish guy who can talk a good fight, but when it comes to the doing of the battle, all too often, there is very little follow through.

All of this new information came crashing down upon me with devastating impact. Not only did I not know what love was, I didn't know how to love in a mature way. It was quite a revelation for a twenty-nine-year-old man with two graduate degrees.

I can remember falling on my knees again and asking God to help me start over. I needed to learn how to become a "lover" in the truest sense of the word.

I have deliberately chosen to begin this book on lovemaking in Christian marriage with learning to be a lover, because I strongly believe this is where mature love in Christian marriage must begin. It may well be that a more behavioristic approach would start somewhere else, but I have chosen to begin here. I believe that each of us must begin with an examination of where we're at and what we're doing. How much have we been "conformed by this world" in our perception of our roles and responsibilities in marriage? How much do we rely on "feelings" only to determine our actions? Do we really know how to love in a mature way? Lovemaking in Christian marriage begins with the relationship and not with techniques and gimmicks. Hopefully, this book will be able to demonstrate how the relationship can make the lovemaking better, and the lovemaking can enrich the relationship.

2

Preparing Your Marriage for Lovemaking

Couples who are successful as lovers are successful not by accident but because they have learned how to communicate. Therefore, any book that would attempt to give advice about lovemaking must include, as its "centerfold," principles that would lead the couple into more effective communication. Yet with all the attention given to the topic of communication, few couples know what communication really is. In fact, communication has become one of the most used yet frequently misunderstood words in the English language—especially as it relates to marriage, and the family.

A young couple who came to me for marriage counseling illustrate the frustration surrounding the issue of communication. During our first session I asked why they had come. Their answer, almost in unison, was "We're just not communicating." Out of curiosity, I asked what they meant when they used the term. After a long pause, the husband shrugged his shoulders and answered, "I guess I really don't know. I only know that whatever it means, we're just not doing it."

The frustration of that young husband is the almost universal cry of modern marriages, "We're just not communicating." For many of us communication has come to imply something we're not doing, the absence of, a mysterious, ill-defined process whose importance is agreed to by everyone yet understood by few. Most of us are hard pressed to explain what it is that "we're not doing."

Part of the problem is that we've made the word too complicated. We've taken something that is basically simple and made it into something that is complex. And then when faced with the "terribly complex" task of communicating with one another we become apprehensive, fearful, and overly sensitive to failure.

Communication in marriage isn't that complicated. It's not difficult; it's just hard work. And most of us tend to shun hard work. It's no wonder we have trouble communicating and as a result have problems in our love life.

In my opinion, communication in marriage takes place when a couple learns to do three things, and to do them faithfully and consistently. In very practical terms there is communication in marriage (1) when the couple learns to communicate their love and care for each other through regular sexual intercourse; (2) when they are spending time with each other, on a daily basis, sharing their lives in a meaningful way; and (3) when they have learned to successfully negotiate their anger and differences constructively and not destructively.

As you can see, according to my definition, communication is a process. It is a process that involves emotions, ranging from the very positive (love and sex) to the very negative (anger and frustration). Successful performance at one end of the continuum, communication sexually, requires successful communication at the other end, the negotiation of anger and frustration. You can't have one without the other. Unfortunately, many Christian couples hoping to relate sexually flounder because they have never learned to argue and manage their anger. "Lovemaking" in its proper context, involves the entire process of communication. This is where lovemaking in a Christian marriage differs from lovemaking in another context. To the Christian, lovemaking is not only a physical act, it is an event. Its deepest meaning is found within the boundaries of the marital relationship and all that goes to make up that relationship. To become a successful lover is to become a person who is able to relate to your partner in the totality of your personality. To skimp or shield your partner from any part of you is to diminish your sexual relationship.

Preparing your marriage for lovemaking, then, requires you to learn the art of communication, and that requires the mastery of some basic skills.

First, it requires learning how to spend time with each other in meaningful interaction and conversation. It is a skill and not something that just "happens." It requires deliberately setting aside time to be with each other—time that is regular, in the sense of being dependable. Many couples successfully manage the "hurt" in their relationship because they know for sure there will be a time and an opportunity to work their problems through.

In contrast, the smallest annoyance in a marriage can become unbearable if it appears it will be there forever. Busy schedules filled with a hundred "important" meetings and appointments can consume every hour until there is little time left in the day or night. We end up trying to go in all directions at once and then wonder why we've lost touch with each other. If you are going to communicate effectively you must set time aside just for that purpose and you must be able to depend upon the other to be there and to carry through with this most important of appointments, your time to communicate. By quality I mean in the sense of *nothing else going on*. It's folly to try to communicate with the television blaring in the background, in between football timeouts, or while the dinner is being prepared. Quality time requires a focus of attention that is impossible to achieve if the slightest distraction persists. Most of us would be shocked if we totaled up the amount of face-to-face time we spent with each other during the last week, the last month, or the last year. Weeks can go by without a meaningful time for the sharing of our lives. In counseling, I have been most successful with those couples who took the time to talk to each other on a dependable, quality basis. The kind of time you spend with each other is very often indicative of how well you are communicating.

There is a third dimension to this "appointment" for communication. It should not only be a time that is dependable, and a time that is quality, it also needs to be a time that is individual—no one else around, especially the children. We sometimes use others as buffers to protect ourselves from the negative reactions we unconsciously fear will be heaped upon us by our "wounded" spouse. Couples who do most of their communicating in front of others and not when they are alone are, in my opinion, really afraid of togetherness and intimacy. Why do many of us tend to avoid face-to-face communication? It is usually because the presence of others inhibits the full disclosure of ourselves to one another, and for many of us full disclosure is a frightening thought. We need to remember that communication involves risk. For some, the risk may involve possible rejection or disapproval. For others, it may touch some fear hidden deep within us. But whatever the risk, the payoff for taking the chance is more than worth it. The payoff is the emotional closeness that results between the two persons. Successful communication and successful lovemaking depend upon the establishment of this emotional closeness. This is what intimacy is all about.

Thus far my emphasis upon communication has been upon the necessity of spending time with each other. Lovers find time to be with each other. But as successful communicators they are able to do something else as well. They have learned to negotiate their anger and their differences in a constructive rather than a destructive manner. Lovemaking requires learning to argue and learning to deal with your anger.

The popular notion that most sexual discouragement in Christian marriage is due to puritanical inhibition is way off base. It's not inhibition that defeats most of us sexually. It's the unresolved anger between us. Anger that has turned to bitterness and hatred. The hurts and bruises that persist in the form of apprehension and fear. When it is time to come close physically, it's almost impossible because we are so far apart emotionally.

What do you do with your anger? When does anger become constructive and not destructive?

To begin to manage their anger and their differences successfully a couple must make a commitment to one another: they must agree to stop their pretense and their lying to one another and to start telling the truth. Truth-telling is what the Apostle Paul encourages believers to do in his letter to the Ephesians. "Therefore, putting away falsehood, let every one speak the truth with his neighbor, for we are members one of another" (Eph. 4:25). If truth-telling is applicable to the relationship between believers, it is certainly applicable between married couples.

The kind of falsehoods the Apostle Paul is talking about is not the blatant lies one tells, but the subtle deception of pretending to be something you're not.

For example, a young husband walks into his house after a long day. He can sense tension in the air. "Is anything wrong? Are you okay?" he asks his wife. Her answer, delivered with appropriate sighing and a martyred tone is, "No I'm all right. It really doesn't matter." But he knows. They've been through this before. He has learned when she's leveling with him and when she's not. He begins to push. "I know when you're upset. Let's have it." They begin to play a game of marital hide and seek. "You're mad." "No I'm not." "Yes you are." And on and on. Many times the confrontation ends up with his labeling her as a martyr and her crawling into a psychological hole. She's hurt because he didn't respond to her in the right way or because he was insensitive.

This kind of lie-telling is one of the most destructive forces in Christian marriage. For some reason,

31

many of us seem to believe that a "good" Christian is always on top of life. One way of handling fear is to deny that you're afraid. If you're angry you smile and pretend you're happy. It doesn't take long in a marriage for the phoniness and the pretense to build. It becomes easier and easier to tell less and less of the truth. Soon, when you need to be able to tell your husband or your wife how you really feel, you can't. You've forgotten how.

I've known many couples in this bind. After years of marriage they are miles apart emotionally and they've lost touch with the realities of how the other feels.

Some couples decide to change. They decide to open up and to let their spouse know what they think, what they feel, what they want, what they like, and don't like. I've seen it time and time again. With the truth comes an unusual benefit: freedom. They begin to experience a quality of openness and freedom in their marriage that they thought would never happen. They can be themselves and not have to be someone else. Where they had feared rejection, they experience acceptance. Where they had anticipated anger, they experience forgiveness. The truth has a way of bringing us closer together.

I have encouraged scores of couples to make a commitment to be open and honest with each other, and not once has a decision to tell the truth proven to be destructive. It must, however, be a decision to *tell the truth in love*.

Suppose a husband has had an affair. His entanglement with the other woman is now over and he has straightened his life out with God. Should he tell his wife that he was involved with another woman? My answer would be yes, if there were additional conditions attached. The additional conditions would have to do with whether or not the "truth" would build or tear down the relationship. Would the truth bring them closer together? The Apostle Paul put the principle this way, "Only let that talk come out of your mouth that is good for edifying, as fits the occasion, that it may impart grace to those who hear" (Eph. 4:29). To edify is to build up. Truthfulness in love involves concerning yourself for the upbuilding of the relationship. If a husband can say with reasonable certainty that telling his wife would make things better, then he should. If he can't say with certainty, then he should be cautious.

There is a second condition to telling the truth. This condition has to do with the appropriate time and place. Paul said truth-telling should "fit the occasion." I think this has to do with timing. There are times to tell the truth and there are times to remain silent, waiting for the appropriate opportunity. Truthfulness shouldn't come out in a hostile context, when there are others present. Speaking the truth in love requires a careful and timely choice of *when* and *where*.

The third condition to telling the truth in love has to do with "imparting grace" to the hearer. Will the truth really benefit him or her as a person? Sometimes the truth can be spoken in such a manner that the hearer feels he or she has been bludgeoned with a meat cleaver. Then again the same issue can be resolved with the skill of a surgeon's knife. The one mutilates and destroys. The other heals.

Truth must be spoken carefully and cautiously, especially if it involves issues such as extramarital affairs. The kind of pain attached to these issues is very real and very intense. It should never be impulsively decided, and should happen only after much thought and counsel.

The second principle that needs to be grasped in order to successfully manage anger, is that anger is a legitimate, God-given emotion designed to accomplish specific purposes within the individual and within our relationships. God the Father gets angry. Jesus was angry (Mark 3:5). Nehemiah in the Old Testament was angry as was Moses and others. In the New Testament the Apostle Paul and others were angry. To say or imply that anger is always sin is to discount the clear teaching of Scripture. What is sin is not the presence of anger, but the failure to handle it properly. We are told to "put away" our anger and not to repress it (Eph. 4:31). The word that is translated "put away" is used elsewhere in Scripture in the sense of "making a clean sweep" (I Cor. 5:2). We are told to "be angry and sin not" (Eph. 4:26). Paul uses a permissive imperative. It could well be translated "When you are angry, don't sin." James encourages us to be "quick to hear, slow to speak and slow to anger" (Jas. 1:19). The Scripture is clear as to the legitimacy of anger as an emotion. What is missing in much of our Christian teaching is the "how" of successfully coping with the anger we are experiencing.

The "how" of anger management is the third principle in this section dealing with communication. A few simple rules, consistently applied, are all that we need to handle anger constructively.

First, we need to learn to communicate about feelings as well as facts. In building bridges of communication both feelings and facts are equally important. For example, suppose a child comes home after school crying. Through the tears the mother learns that the child feels that his teacher doesn't like him and is picking on him. His mother can accept his feelings and validate them, even though she knows that they are not based on the actual facts. A recounting of the facts, to the child, without first accepting his feelings has the effect of discounting his feelings. And soon he will learn not to express them.

Applying the principle to my marriage, if my wife is angry with me, irrespective of the reason, her anger is valid. It may not be accurate, but it is valid. When communicating about anger we must begin with the feelings before moving on to the facts. I need to admit to myself and to my "anger object" that I am angry as the first step toward resolving it. She, in turn, needs to accept the presence of my anger as being real and then wait for the next step.

Second, in the expression of my anger, I need to learn to be assertive with my feelings and not aggressive. Assertiveness, according to my definition, is the ability to speak the truth about my feelings without punishing others with them. Aggressiveness, on the other hand, involves the use of my feelings in a punitive way. It is hitting the other person with my words. To be assertive is to say, "I'm feeling uncared for." It is, "I'm upset because the house is messed up again." It's not, "You're the lousiest housekeeper I've ever known." It's, "I can't seem to get my point across to you and I'm frustrated." It's not, "You're too stupid. It's no wonder I can't communicate with you." Assertiveness invites reflection and consideration, whereas aggressiveness invites defensiveness and retaliation. More of us would be able to communicate our angry feelings effectively if we would only learn to be assertive and not aggressive.

Third, I need to learn to stay with one issue and to stay with it until there is some sort of resolution, rather than stacking issues and then leaving them unresolved. Most conflict in marriage is unproductive because we fail to identify the one issue we are going to argue about. Soon we've got as many as ten issues in the pot all at the same time. Finally, we agree about number ten but because of all the unresolved emotion attached to issues one through nine, we leave the scene of the argument feeling that nothing has been accomplished. We then conclude that anger and argument never really get us anywhere. Instead we should conclude that we have mismanaged our anger and that we need to learn to talk about one issue at a time. If need be we should write it down on a three-by-five card and refer to it during the course of our argument. Most of us will be surprised how quickly we stray from home base.

In the same way, we need to stay with our argument until we've worked it through. But this is hard. The reason it's hard is that all of us have a psychological mechanism inside our being that warns us when we are getting angrier than we *ought* to get. The "ought" is determined by the level of anger we were allowed to express when we were growing up. For some of us the "ought" level is very low because we were never allowed to get angry. And now, as adults, when our anger begins to reach the "ought" level a buzzer goes off inside that yells "don't you dare go any farther." We then withdraw or bail out. A wife runs from the room hysterically throwing herself across the bed, or a husband storms out of the house yelling, "I don't want to talk about it anymore." What the participants in an argument need to realize is that many times our "ought" anger levels are set so low as to keep us from getting anything resolved. As a solution we need to agree that no matter what we say or do at the moment we will try our best to come back and pick the issue up at the same place. You'll be surprised how many arguments are nearly resolved only to be prematurely terminated. If you can hang in there beyond the time you want to bail out, most often a state of reasonableness follows the anger. The problem is that most of us don't stay with it long enough.

The last rule you need to remember in arguing is probably the most important. Winning is not the purpose of an argument. The purpose of an argument is to communicate through the negotiation of your differences, with the emphasis upon negotiation. Winning usually necessitates the loss of someone's personal integrity. Negotiation does not. Winning requires that someone lose. Negotiation does not. No one likes to be a loser and if in your marriage one of you usually wins and the other usually loses, the pattern will be established at the expense of the loser. The irony of most win or lose arguments is that the more verbally powerful partner usually wins whether or not he or she is right. Learning to argue and to manage your anger requires you to learn to negotiate.

You can learn to negotiate in the midst of your arguments by learning to say to yourself, "What is he or she really trying to say to me?" This question when raised at the right time will force you to crawl into your partner's skin and feel what he or she is feeling. The question calls forth empathy, and empathy is at the center of negotiation. Every argument can be negotiated successfully when—and only when—you are convinced your partner really understands what you are trying to say. All of us have experienced the end of an argument when everything is still left hanging, when there is a feeling that it is not over. At the heart of that unsettled feeling is the sometimes unconscious awareness that you have not been understood. In contrast, you can finish a confrontation in which you obviously don't win but still feel that something was accomplished. That "something" is the feeling that you have been understood.

You prepare your marriage for lovemaking by learning the art and the skill of communication. It is a process that must be learned. It is a process that requires work, time and effort. It requires a quality of perseverance and determination. It can be terribly discouraging and it can be rewarding. So hang in there.

3

Preparing Your Wife for Lovemaking

What kind of husband is a Christian wife most likely to be attracted to sexually? Many men would give a year's salary if only they could get their wives to be more sexually responsive, or at least that's what many of them would like to think. They would like to believe that the sexual problems in their marriages are really "her fault." That way they're off the hook. I have already suggested that the key to a healthy, normal sex life in Christian marriage lies within the boundaries of the relationship. It lies within the nature of the relationship and the kind of people we are for one another—and the emphasis is upon "for one another." The importance of the "for one another" has been clearly defined in God's portrait of a Christian husband and confirmed by recent secular scholarship as well. The Scripture is in Paul's letter to the Ephesians, chapter five, and the scholarship is a study by Dr. Seymour Fisher of the State University of New York. Dr. Fisher investigated the differences between women who were high and those who were low in sexual responsiveness.[1]

Dr. Fisher's research involved middle-class married women whose sexual feelings and fantasies were minutely examined. The women were asked to provide information about many different aspects of their sexuality. Inquiries were made about such matters as techniques by which orgasm is attained, feelings during and after orgasm, foreplay, intercourse conditions favoring achievement of orgasm, etc. In addition to the sexual dimension itself, Dr. Fisher investigated, in detail, his subjects' social and psychological makeup. Traits, attitudes, and values were examined using techniques that probed at both the conscious and unconscious levels. What evolved was a thorough and well documented study of female sexuality. The conclusions of his study provide the careful reader with insights into what helps and what hinders a woman's sexual responsiveness. The information is of immeasurable help for a husband who wants to prepare his wife for lovemaking.

One of the findings of the study was that the traditional explanations for the differences between the high and the low orgasmic female were of very little usefulness. For example, traditional Freudian psychoanalytic theory proved to be totally inadequate in explaining the differences. According to Freudian theory, the woman who cannot reach orgasm is psychologically flawed. It is said that she is "struggling with unconscious conflicts which make her anxious and unstable." Instead, Dr. Fisher found that "mental health (emotional stability) and orgasm capacity

[1] Seymour Fisher, *Understanding the Female Orgasm* (New York: Bantam Books, 1973).

simply cannot be equated." What this means to the woman who is struggling with her sexual responsiveness is that she need no longer feel "inadequate," "emotionally immature," or "psychologically unstable." In fact, dwelling upon the psychological side of the issue probably aggravates her problem and feeds her unresponsiveness. The answers to her sexual problems more likely than not lie in what is happening between her and her sexual partner and not what is happening inside her mind.

For purposes of our discussion, Dr. Fisher's study identified two major insights into the nature of female orgasmic capacity.

In the first place, orgasm capacity in a woman is very strongly tied to her perceptions and feelings concerning the dependability of her relationships with the significant people in her life. The study indicated that the highly orgasmic woman has the ability to trust the people in her life in general and the men in particular. The men will be there when they are needed. They are dependable. They are seen to be the kind of men that look after a woman's best interests. In contrast, the woman who is low in orgasm capacity is characterized by a fear of loss of significant relationships. According to Dr. Fisher:

> In essence, then, she might be said to view herself as lacking *dependable* attachment to people who really count. Her anxiety about loss may then be converted into real alarm when, in the course of building up sexual excitement, she finds that objects become perceptually hazy and seem to be "slipping away."

She finds it difficult to trust and to depend on others. As a result, if something has to get done, she does it herself. In the extreme, her feelings could be expressed in the phrase "give a man half-a-chance and he'll let you down." The psychological impact is that the low-orgasmic woman instinctively feels that the significant people in her life will either go away or let her down so therefore she can't depend on them. She has to stand on her own two feet. She finds it difficult to trust, to relax, to abandon herself into the arms of her lover, and as a result her apprehension robs her body of its ability to fully respond sexually.

The second major finding of Dr. Fisher's study has to do with the quality of her relationship that existed between the woman and her father. Again, the study found with reliable consistency that:

> the lower a woman's orgasm capacity the more likely she is to describe her father as having treated her "casually," without elaborate attempts at control or enforcing his will, as having been easygoing rather than expecting conformity to well-defined rules. To put it another way, the greater a woman's orgasm capacity, the less permissive and the more controlling she perceives her father to be.

In his attempt to explain this finding Dr. Fisher suggests that the significant male in a woman's early years sets the pattern, the tone, which will greatly influence her expectations for the significant male in her married years. She comes, unconsciously, to see the passive relationships with significant males in her life as evidence that they "really don't care" or else they would be more involved with her. She expects a quality of distance to characterize her relationships.

In contrast, the woman whose father was involved, interested, and who invested himself in her learns very early that a man can really care what happens to her. She learns that she needs to work, to perform, to respond to the significant male in her life. Later, when she marries the pattern has been established. She is accustomed to the expectation of responding to a man.

In summary, Dr. Fisher's study points out two basic facts which undergird a woman's orgasm capacity. First, the more dependable, caring, and trusting her relationship is with her lover the greater will be her ability to reach orgasm sexually. Second, the more involved, expecting, and standard-setting her lover is the greater will be her ability to reach orgasm sexually.

With these two basic facts in mind we need to look to the Scripture to see what kind of a man God encourages the Christian husband to be. In particular I think God's portrait of a Christian husband found in Paul's letter to the Ephesians, 5:22-33, hits the issue right on the head. I'm convinced that the kind of man described by Paul is very much the kind of man that is most likely to draw strong, healthy sexual response from his wife by meeting the same basic needs Dr. Fisher identified in his study. What kind of man is he?

First, the Christian husband is encouraged "to love his wife as Christ also loved the church and gave himself up for her" (verse 25). The Christian *husband is encouraged to be the kind of man who loves his wife with a giving, sacrificing, kind of love.*

This kind of love is a very practical, visible kind of love. It's a love that provides a certain sure foundation upon which a wife can depend. But it's not an easy kind of love to actually do.

If you're like me, just thinking about this kind of love almost defeats you. Why? Because most of the time when we should be sacrificing, we're selfish. When we should be giving, we're taking. When we should be kind, we're harsh. Becoming a sacrificing kind of lover requires more than we have in us to become. How in the world can the dilemma be resolved?

Thinking in terms of "love currency" has been helpful to me. Suppose, for example, you were living in the United States and your wife lived in Japan. Goods and services are purchased in the United States using dollars. In Japan those same goods and services can be purchased using Japanese yen. If you were to try to purchase a gift for your wife while the two of you were in Japan, your dollars would be useless. You would need to go through a currency exchange process converting your dollars into yen. Then your purchasing power would be the same. Going into a store and demanding they take your dollars would only brand you as an "ugly" American. You're too smart for that. When in Japan you need to barter and trade using their medium of exchange.

So it is with love. Each person has a "love currency" all his own. A husband might do something for his wife that to him is the essence of "sacrifice" only to find that it meant very little to her. Why? Because he failed to translate his actions into her currency. To him, love might mean an expensive gift or exotic trip. To her, love means quality time spent with her doing the things that are important to her. To him, love is taking her along on a business trip. To her, love is finishing the landscaping in the backyard. In order for a husband to learn to love with a sacrificial kind of love he has to learn the skill of converting his actions into deeds that make her feel loved and valued. Most of us love others in ways that make us feel loved, not them. The art of loving a wife sacrificially involves doing for her what she will experience as love.

This brings me to the second dimension of the portrait: *the need of a Christian woman to have a husband whose life is an example to her*. The Apostle Paul says that the Lord Jesus "cleansed" the church by the "washing of water with the word" (verse 26). What did he mean? As we look back on what Jesus did for us, we think not only of his death on the cross but also of the quality of his life. Whenever we talk about goodness, holiness, and righteousness we often think of Jesus. The kind of person Jesus was and the quality of life he lived has set an example for Christians of all ages. So it is to be in the relationship between a Christian husband and his wife. The Christian wife, irrespective of how spiritually strong or weak she is, needs a husband who is really trying in his relationship with God. He's taking it seriously. What I'm suggesting is that part of the dysfunctional relationship that exists in many Christian marriages can be traced to the failure of the husband to establish his own sense of holiness before God. He may struggle and he may fail but what she needs is to see that he is trying. What is important to her is that he has taken his place as a spiritual leader in his own home. He is a leader by way of example.

In my experience as a marriage counselor I have

seen it happen time and time again. When a husband says to his wife, and to me, "I'm wrong. I've not been what I ought to be in my relationship with God. All that I can promise is that I'll try," things begin to change. For the first time the wife begins to look at her husband through different eyes. He becomes the kind of person whom she can respect. He begins to earn the right to be responded to. He becomes a significant standard-setting male in her life.

Dr. Fisher's research only identified what many women have known for years. A woman's respect for her husband magnifies her ability to respond to him sexually consistently over time. If she doesn't respect him on rare occasions she can conjure up some kind of sexual response through a combination of fantasy, and because it's the right time of the month and her hormones are cooperating. But the real test comes at the other times of the month, when she may not "feel" as sexy. At those times she needs more than her raw instincts. She needs someone she "wants" to respond to, someone she "wants" to please. It becomes difficult to respond to someone for whom she feels disgust or disrespect. She just isn't made that way and the Christian husband needs to realize it. Perhaps this is what the Apostle Paul meant when he told the Corinthian church that "the wife does not have (exclusive) authority and control over her own body, but the husband (has his rights)" (I Cor. 7:4). A husband needs to be reminded that the kind of person he is and the kind of relationship he has with God is directly related to the kind of *"authority and control"* he has over his wife's body. She needs his help to "turn her on." His responsiveness to God helps her be responsive to him.

This brings me to the third dimension in the portrait of the Christian husband. *A Christian wife needs a husband who will love her with a "nourishing," "cherishing," kind of love.* Again I'd like to point out a parallel between Scripture and Dr. Fisher's research. He suggested that a woman who is sexually responsive to the point of regularly having orgasm tends to have a father who was an active, standard-setting participant in her life. He tended to be a person who was involved in what was important to her and that involvement was taken to mean that he really cared and loved her. It's not by accident that the Scripture teaches that when the love object in a woman's life is no longer the father but a husband, that her husband is to care for her with a special kind of love. A love from which she can derive sustenance, a kind of spiritual, social, emotional kind of food, a "nourishing" kind of love.

Most men begin marriage with a terrible disadvantage—they were raised by mothers. By that I mean many mothers, often good Christian mothers, tend to spoil their sons to the point that they never really learn to be responsible for or to a woman. Sons are often taught to take from women and rarely to give. Many sons learn that when they're done with a towel, don't fold it, stuff it in the rack. Are their clothes dirty? Take them off and leave them in a pile. Never! Never! Never, pick them up and put them in the clothes hamper. That's mother's work. They learn to be "takers" and not "givers." When they marry, they do so with the expectation that their wife will carry on where their mothers left off—seeing to it that she meets his needs whatever they might happen to be. Seeing to it that she nourishes him and rarely vice versa. That's the tragedy. Who nourishes the wife if the husband doesn't?

Nourishment involves becoming conscious that your wife is a total person who would like you to become a significant 'other' to her in much of what she does, says, and feels. I'm amazed how many husbands can clearly define what their needs are but stumble when it comes to the definition of their wife's needs. For example, a young wife who is boxed in by the demands of her pre-school children during the day hungers for an intelligent conversation with her husband when he returns at night, but all she gets from him is a meaningless grunt as he passes through the kitchen on the way to the den and Monday night football. A wife in her middle years, children gone, with hours to fill during the day aches for an invitation to lunch from her busy executive husband. Instead he takes a client, a friend, or sometimes his secretary. The wife is left at home with the expectation that she "understand." She has needs but no one to fill them so she turns elsewhere, to jobs, to clubs, to church, sometimes to other men.

What seems to me to be the issue is the stark reality that many husbands have abandoned the responsibility of being an active, involved presence in their wife's spiritual, social, emotional, and intellectual existence. What she really needs is a total diet served up by a loving, concerned husband who is aware of her needs, her wants, her goals as a person. Husbands need to be reminded that marriage is a two-way street, from "me to her" as well as from "her to me." She must have "nourishment." She'll find it somewhere.

This brings me to the fourth and last dimension in Paul's portrait of a Christian husband. *A Christian wife needs a "cherishing" kind of love.* By this I mean that a wife needs her husband to value her above all else, except God. It's very easy for a woman to come to the place where she feels used and unimportant. Oftentimes a Christian husband who would never think of having an affair with another woman will instead have "an affair" with his job, with a hobby, or even the local church. For the Christian husband the church is an especially seductive mistress.

In my opinion, service in the local church is not always synonymous with service for Christ. I am amazed at the number of earnestly committed Christian men who would never forsake their wives for another woman but instead forsake their wives and their families for the building committee, the deacon board, midweek visitation and whatever else happens to be going on. Let me carefully say what I mean. The same Bible that challenges a man to love God with all his heart, soul, mind and strength, also enjoins him to "provide for those in his own house." To provide for your family involves more than the provision of food and shelter. It involves your active concerned participation in their lives, especially your wife's. If a husband doesn't, he's judged by God to be worse than an infidel (I Tim. 5:8). Even pastors who are challenged by God to leave all and follow Christ are also challenged to "rule and care for their own households well" (I Tim. 3:4–5). Serving Christ in a scriptural sense of the concept never results in the neglect of one's marriage or family.

When there is neglect, in my opinion, it is because we are serving something or someone else (our own ego needs or the approval of others). It is not because we are serving God.

The difficulty to love in this way is illustrated by my own experience. On one particular occasion I had sat down at the dinner table for the evening meal. I sat at one end of the table, my two daughters to my left, and my wife at the other end of the table directly opposite me. I had every confidence that the meal would be excellent as usual. My wife had prepared a pepper steak that is one of my favorites and had placed the plate full of meat immediately to my right. I had taken a piece of meat and had passed the plate to my eldest daughter. Without hesitation she asked a question that God used to shake me to my very foundations. "Daddy, why do you always take the biggest piece?" Earlier that day or the day before my wife had complained that I had been neglecting her but I had brushed her complaint aside as the dripping of a nagging wife. But this time my daughter, although indirectly, had agreed. Why indeed do I always take the biggest piece? I mumbled some sort of answer to my daughter and went on with the meal. Afterward I went for a walk. The coolness of the night air cleared my head and exposed my selfishness. I saw myself in a light that was most revealing. I now understood what was happening. With knee-jerk habit I was always serving myself first. My children were following suit and serving their needs and whatever was left over was supposed to be enough to suffice my wife. But it wasn't. She had said it many times in different words but I wasn't listening. She needed me to care for her. This time, however, I heard and decided to try to do something different.

The next night I laid out my plans in advance. After the table was set in its typical pattern with my wife at the opposite end of the table, I moved my wife's plate to my immediate right. When she brought the main dish and set it down she noticed the difference but said nothing, returning to the kitchen for the rest of the food. This time things were to be different. I deliberately served her first with the best of everything. The kids immediately caught on and wanted to be served too. I simply answered that she was my wife and deserved for me to take care of her but that I hadn't been doing a very good job and hoped to do better. The best was yet to come. My wife rounded the corner from the kitchen to the dining room and saw what had happened. The smile that erupted on her face could have lit up the house. She knew and she understood. Finally her husband was catching on. Someone was going to be looking after her.

A wife needs her husband to be responsive to her needs sometimes at his own expense. Perhaps this is what Dr. Fisher's study touched upon. The need in a woman to have a caring, "cherishing" kind of lover. The hope that her husband, her lover, will put the satisfaction of her needs before the satisfaction of his own.

In this one-flesh relationship called marriage it's very easy for a woman to feel like an object and not like a person. In order for that not to happen she needs a husband who helps her to feel privileged, cherished, and valued. "You are important to me" is what a wife needs to hear from her husband, and said with both words and actions.

If I am a Christian husband and sexually my marriage is not really what it could or should be, it's easy to lay the responsibility for the problems at my wife's feet. "Well, it's all your fault. If it weren't for your unresponsiveness things would be a lot better." I think the weight of both Scripture and modern scientific research bears out the fact that the place I need to begin is not only with her but also with me. Am I the kind of husband she needs me to be? Does what I provide for her in our relationship help or hinder me as I prepare her for lovemaking?

4

Preparing Your Husband for Lovemaking

It never ceases to amaze me that women who are sexually attractive to their husbands come in such different sizes and shapes. Recently, at a Christian camp, I was talking with a well-satisfied husband who was describing his wife to me. My morning message had been about sex and in our discussion the verbal images he outlined dealing with the success of their sex life would have made most of us envious. "I can't imagine how any woman could be more exciting in bed than she is. She has learned how to turn me on so easily that it's embarrassing some times." It was obvious that he could go on forever. He was happy with her and he was deliriously happy with the marriage. Without thinking, I immediately conjured up in my mind the image of a ravenously beautiful seductress "on the make." The epitome of the "total woman." Then she walked up, and my images crumbled. She was short, flat chested, and a bit on the homely side. I expected him to refer to her as "Sis" but he didn't. She was his lover, and as she approached you could tell that she was a "beautiful woman." I must have looked confused because after he shyly told her about our conversation she chuckled and said to me, "you look surprised," and I was. All of my confusion was removed within five minutes as I watched the love flow between them. She was truly a beautiful woman whose beauty depended not on the size of her breasts nor in her skill in making up her face. Her beauty depended upon the grace of her person. She felt good about herself inside and whatever she lacked physically the loveliness of her inner self more than made up for it. I had to excuse myself and return to a meeting and as they walked away arm in arm she playfully nudged him with her hip and he affectionately responded by patting her on the rear. I remember wishing I could bottle whatever she had and give it away to all of the Christian wives I know who are struggling with feeling good about themselves and feeling good about their sexuality. She had learned a secret and together they were enjoying its benefits.

What kind of wife is a Christian husband most likely to be attracted to sexually? Most Christian husbands are like any other kind of man. They want a well-proportioned (usually referring to breast and waist size), attractive, and seductive kind of woman who is ready and available for sex at any time of day or night. This may sound crass and carnal but I'm convinced it's not far removed from what many Christian wives think their husbands are looking for. But is this what a Christian husband *really* wants? Does he want a "pussycat" (to use Elaine Stedman's term) who meets him at the door "ready for action?" That may not be bad for a change of pace but what about the rest of the week, the month, the year? Not as a prevailing style of life.

Most Christian husbands don't want their wives to model themselves after the *Playboy* or *Penthouse* centerfold. That kind of image fits in a magazine but it doesn't fit into life. It certainly doesn't fit in the lives of couples who are taking their walk with Christ seriously. Let me explain why I feel so strongly about this approach to sexuality in Christian marriage.

The problems I have with *Playboy* and *Penthouse* are not the typical ones. It's not the pictures and the nudity that bother me. What really bothers me is the underlying philosophy and life-style they represent, especially as they define human sexuality. Human sexuality is removed from the context of loving, caring, and enduring relationships. Sex is represented as a "do it now" physical act rather than the union of two people into one and whose oneness persists over time. Their emphasis degrades sexuality and in the long run diminishes it. I'm convinced that when sex is placed in the broader context of lovemaking, and lovemaking is placed in the broader context of communication in a total human relationship, sex is magnified and not diminished.

However, the Playboy philosophy has gained widespread acceptance for a reason. As Christians we need to be asking ourselves why. Of all people, Christians should have the healthiest and the most robust view of human sexuality. But instead of being free, many of us are sexually bound. In reaction to our uptightness the world has sought other alternatives. We have deeded the area of human sexuality over to the world and into the void the world has inserted its value system. It's time for us to take a positive attitude toward our sexuality rather than a negative one. A Christian view of sexuality when lived to its fullest is an alternative to Playboyism and "pussycatism."

Somewhere between the high-collared Victorian prude and the impish "curled on the fur rug" groupie, is a middle ground that allows a woman to be all that she can be sexually and still be consistent with her Christian values. The search for that middle ground is the task faced by the wife who would be sexually attractive for her Christian husband.

I mentioned earlier that often God reveals truth to us that is deeply insightful into the nature of human personality and human relationships. Just as he speaks in the New Testament as to the basic needs of Christian wives, so does he speak in the New Testament as to the basic needs of Christian husbands. In Peter's first letter, God has instructed the Christian wife to be a certain kind of person. The young wife I mentioned earlier had·mined the truth of Scripture and was spending the profit in her marriage. Her husband was pleased with the results. What were the secrets she had discovered?

That young wife had learned to look into Scripture for the principles upon which to build her life. It's interesting to me that the result of her search was to become liberated both personally and sexually. She had learned to apply the principles found in Peter's first letter, chapter three.

The first principle she had learned is that *a Christian husband needs his wife to be responsive to his leadership.* I've come to the conclusion that this is the essence of the meaning of submission. There is in each of us, both men and women, a need to be valued and trusted. When a man marries, his assumption of the role of husband brings certain responsibilities. He is responsible to society for his performance in that role. If he is a Christian, he is responsible to God as well. There is deep within the gut of a Christian husband the knowledge that God would have him to be a certain kind of person and a certain kind of husband. He needs to function in the role of "Christian husband" as God defines it. A wife who is responsive to her husband makes his task easier rather than harder. She needs to be "submissive" to him, that is, responsive to his leadership.

Before developing this point any further, it's important that we understand what "submission" means in the biblical sense of the word.

To begin with, submission is *the voluntary response of one partner to another*. Whatever it means, it doesn't mean coercion. It is not the imposition of the will of one partner upon the other. Let's create a hypothetical situation by way of illustration.

A Christian couple has returned home after an evening out. They are sitting in their car discussing their life and problems when the wife's discontent begins to surface.

"My life is just plain dull. I'm tired of going to meetings only to come home to the same chores. I need a change."

"What do you want to do?" her husband answers, priding himself at his openness.

"I think I want to go back to work." Her response lands like a bombshell between them. "Why? Because he likes having her home and he thinks the kids do too.

"That's out of the question. You'll just have to work your frustrations out some other way."

"You can't mean that. That makes me think you don't care how I feel."

"I care. I just don't want you going back to work."

"Not even if that's what would make me happy?"

"Don't try to twist what I'm trying to say. I'm only saying that you should stay at home if I decide that's what you should do. After all, there is such a thing as the chain of command. Isn't there?"

Her frustration turns to hurt and she finds herself boxed in. He has "pulled rank" on her invoking the ultimate in authority. "The chain of command." If she continues to object she is guilty of insubordination to her "head" so she must swallow her feelings and continue on with her frustrating life-style. There is no appeal. The final word has been spoken.

The words and the situations change from couple to couple but the issue remains the same. A wife is to do as she is told whether she likes it or not. Some commands come in the form of quiet orders. Others come in the form of bellowed ultimatums. What is consistent is that the husband always has the last word. The wife must always do as she is told.

I think that this approach is inconsistent with the will of God because it isn't biblical. Why do I say this? Because of the example of submission of Jesus, the Son of God, to his Father. Biblical submission has been modeled for us in the relationship between the Son and the Father.

We are told in Scripture that Jesus was submissive to his Father in everything, (John 17:4) and his submission was voluntary. Never was he coerced to do anything. Had he been forced to do the will of the Father, his response would have been meaningless. By application, if a wife is to submit to her husband she is to do so voluntarily. Even when he feels strongly about an issue he must give her the freedom to make up her own mind and not try to make it up for her.

What makes this kind of relationship difficult is that the husband must give up his absolute power. He can no longer dictate. He must negotiate. In giving up his absolute control over his wife he gains something in return, the voluntary acquiescence of a willing partner. She is free to be herself and free to respond to him.

Submission in Christian marriage is not only to be voluntary, it is also to be a *decision between equals*. It is not the surrender of an inferior to a superior. One of the detriments of the "chain of command" interpretation of submission is that in its practical application the wife usually becomes the traditional doormat, the enlisted "man" obeying the orders of the "commanding" officer. I have concluded that whatever submission means, the meaning has to be applicable to the relationship that exists between the members of the Trinity.

Jesus submitted to the will of the Father but he was never an inferior. Although he became human, he still had claim to equality (John 17:5; Philippians 2:6). His submissiveness did not alter his equality. As it is in the relationship between the members of the Trinity, so it is to be in the relationship between the Christian couple who have become "one flesh." The members of the Godhead are one and they are equals and so are husbands and wives. They are one and they are equal.

In addition to voluntariness and equality is an even more important facet of the meaning of submission. It is that *submission in Christian marriage is to be mutual*. It is not to be a one-way street with the wife always submitting to the husband and the husband "commanding" the wife. The mutuality of submission is conveniently forgotten by those interpreters who would enforce a rigid "chain of command."

The Apostle Paul in the book of Ephesians 5:21 instructs Christians to "be subject to one another out of reverence for Christ." The emphasis is upon the reciprocity of the relationship. Immediately following he does reiterate that wives are to be in subjection to their husbands, possibly because it's so easy for them not to be. But the primary point is that submission means it is mutual. I have suggested that submission means "to be responsive to the leadership of another." If submission is to be mutual, it would mean that there are areas in our family life where I am the leader and there are areas where my wife is the leader. There are times when we defer to one another.

The principle of mutuality of submissiveness in marriage is similar to the pattern of submissiveness between the members of the Body of Christ. There are times in the Body when it is appropriate for one member to exercise leadership over the other members as a function of his or her spiritual gift (I Corinthians 12:14–26). No single spiritual gift automatically qualifies a member to be the leader or ultimate decision maker all of the time. That position belongs to the Head, Jesus himself. Likewise in marriage, in which there is mutuality of submissiveness, the role of leadership is assigned not according to some decree from God or on the basis of the leadership role the partner has been assigned by the mutual decision of the marriage. The skill of a Christian marriage lies in the negotiation and assignment of these leadership roles on the basis of the abilities of the partners.

How do you decide who is going to lead when there is an obvious disagreement? In most Christian marriages (following the "chain of command"), the husband decides. But is this right? Is it biblical? I think not. If there is anything clear in Scripture it is that the privileges and glories of leadership are not to be grasped and jealously held on to. That was the clear example of the Lord Jesus (Philippians 2:6–8). Also, the grasping and clinging to the glories of leadership were the errors of the Christians at Philippi. Because of their error the Apostle Paul encouraged each of them to submit themselves one to another and to "do nothing from selfishness and conceit, but in humility count others better than yourselves. Let each of you look not only to his own interests, but also to the interests of others" (Philippians 2:3–4). Leadership in Christian marriage, like leadership in the Body of Christ, is therefore not something to be grasped and clung to. It is something to be given away, trusting ultimately to the leadership or headship of Jesus himself.

I believe the negotiation of leadership roles in marriage is one of the most difficult issues for many of us to work through. The tendency is always to operate at the extremes. Either the husband is always passive, leaving the responsibilities of leadership to the wife or he is always dominant, leaving the role of follower perpetually to the wife. In either case, friction and dissatisfaction usually result.

Lovemaking, like submission, has to be mutual to be successful. There are times when it is entirely appropriate for the wife to be the leader and to seduce her husband. However, if she has been as-

signed the perpetual role of follower in most of the
other interactions with her husband, it becomes
next to impossible for her to suddenly become the
leader or aggressor in their sexual relationship. In
the same way, if she must always be the leader because of the passivity of her husband it is difficult
to abandon herself sexually to someone she is unac-
customed to responding to. It works best when it
is mutual.

The resolution of the submissiveness issue is vitally
related to the quality of the lovelife of a Christian
couple. The ideal is for them to be willing partners
in the mutual give and take of lovemaking. One
leading now. Another leading later. The variety
and creativity of the relationship combine to make
them desire one another even more. "For the wife
does not rule over her own body but the husband
does; likewise the husband does not rule over his
own body but the wife does" (I Corinthians 7:4).
We are to look after our partner's interests seeing
to it that their needs are met before our own. We
are to submit ourselves one to another.

Returning to the mainstream of the chapter, the
Apostle Peter includes a rather interesting statement in his discussion of submissiveness. He says,
"Likewise you wives be submissive to your husbands, so that some, though they do not obey the
word, may be won without a word by the behavior
of their wives" (1 Peter 3:1). Peter's advice is
directed to those wives whose husbands are disobedient to the Lord. The natural tendency for
many wives caught in this position is to become
"spokeswomen" for God. In the earnest desire to see
their husbands drawn to God they very often accomplish the exact opposite. Their words get in the way

of the still, quiet voice of the Holy Spirit as he speaks to their husbands.

Years ago I remember talking to a very dedicated Christian woman who found herself in this situation. Her husband was not a Christian and refused to have anything to do with the things of God. Her relationship with God was just the opposite. She really loved the Lord. Unfortunately, she equated activity with dedication. Whenever the doors of the church were open she was there. She was president of this group and chairwoman of that committee. She couldn't get enough. Day after day she was at the church "working for God." However, the problem wasn't her days. The problem was her nights. She felt very strongly that she should participate in the services of the church on both Wednesday and Sunday nights. Every time she left the house in the evening to attend church her husband became a little more angry until the whole issue had grown into a major problem. She was convinced that her faithfulness in attending church was a form of witness and that she ought to go. In contrast, her husband had come to see her involvement in church as an indication that she was neglecting the family. In my conversation with him he dwelt upon the damaging effects it was having upon the children but I could see that beneath the surface he felt she was neglecting him. Her first attempts to entice him to go to church with her took the form of gentle requests. But as the weeks and the months went by her requests had turned to nagging and eventually hardened into defiance. She had come to me as a counselor out of desperation because the night before he had threatened to leave her if she didn't stay at home and when home she was to "shut her mouth" about God. It wasn't difficult for me as an objective third party to see that she desperately wanted her husband to come to Christ but instead was driving him away. We talked about the effect her nagging was having upon him. I then turned to the third chapter of Peter's letter and read the first verse. She had never noticed that she is instructed to be submissive to her disobedient husband and to demonstrate that submissiveness by being quiet. In return, the Lord gave her a promise, to bring her husband to Christ. I can still see her amazement as she read and reread the words. "It is a promise, isn't it." "Yes," I answered. "And your step of faith is to believe that if you are quiet and leave the conviction to the Holy Spirit, God promises to eventually bring your husband to himself."

Later in the week I learned that she had returned home and had apologized to her husband for her attitude and negotiated a compromise with him. He agreed to go with her to church on Sunday mornings if she agreed to stay at home with him and the children the rest of the week. Their negotiated settlement removed most of the tensions in their marriage. I've since lost touch but the last time I saw them they were in the parking lot of the church on a Sunday morning walking to their car. I could tell by the laughter and animation that filled their conversation that things were better between them. I'm sure that God has or will keep his part of the bargain as well.

There is a second basic need that is present in a Christian husband. It is *the need to be respected as a person and not to be manipulated.*

We live in a world in which respect is a diminishing commodity. In no other area is this loss of respect more prevalent than in the area of marriage. I have spoken before scores of women's groups in which during the question and answer period there is a recurring theme: their husbands' loss of respect for them. Wives who feel they are useless and are being treated as objects. The women's magazines abound with the trumpet call to women to assert their rights and demand they be treated as persons and not things. And they're right. But there is another side to the coin. I cringe when I see or hear the attitudes of some women toward their husbands. "My husband is a lazy slob. If there is a job to do he'll try to get out of it every time." Or, "All my husband wants is sex. If I want to get anything out of him I just need to spend a few minutes in bed and then I usually can get him to do most anything I want." This is overt disrespectfulness.

There is, in my opinion, an even more destructive tendency afoot today. It is the covert disrespectfulness of many of the popular books written to the Christian woman. The underlying theme of many of the popular books for Christian women on the market today is that men are to be manipulated. If the woman acts in the right way or does the right thing she can get her husband to treat her the way she's always wanted. She can get him to give her what she's yearned for. The irony of this approach is that it treats the husband like an object. This is the exact opposite of what women are saying they are trying to rid themselves of. If one is wrong, so is the other.

Suppose, for example, a wife wants her husband to help her more around the house. There are projects that have gone unattended for months. How can she get him to act? Some "experts" would have the wife start to do the projects herself and do a clumsy job in the process. When he sees how inept she is he will intervene. At that time the wife is to fuss over him in such a way as to make him feel necessary and important. It seems to me that what this approach is doing is to assume that a man is a little boy to be fooled into doing what his "mommy" wants him to do. She of course knows best. That isn't respect as I see it. It's the exact opposite. It's deceit and manipulation in its strongest form.

But what is respect? Both the Apostle Paul and the Apostle Peter touch on the subject. Paul in Ephesians 5:33 says, "Let the wife see that she respects her husband," and Peter counsels wives to live their lives in such a way that their husbands "see your reverent and chaste behavior" (1 Peter 3:2). Respectful behavior on the part of a wife for her husband is to live her life in such a way as to be open and honest with him.

Respectful, open, and honest behavior of a wife toward her husband is even more effective than manipulation. How do I know? Because I've seen it happen in my own marriage.

Immediately after I graduated from seminary and had taken a position on the staff of a large church, my wife and I came upon financial hard times. Our bills had piled up to the point where they weren't getting paid on time. On top of that, I had been paying the bills and had managed to mess our check book up so badly that we had checks bouncing all over Southern California. In the midst of the crisis we sat down at the kitchen table and made a number of decisions. The first was that my wife would manage the money. (At the time it was necessary. We have since divided the chore.) We also decided that neither of us would spend any money for whatever reason except for the basic necessities, such as food, utilities, and gas for the car. We had a plan and we both agreed to it. Then, without my knowledge, my wife spent some money. She came upon a shoe store that was having a sale and she loves shoes. She went in to look and came out the owner of two pair. By the time she got home her conscience was raking her over the coals. "What about your agreement with Dennis?" She hid the shoes in the deepest recesses of her closet and let a day go by. What should she do? She could have found a way to get me to agree. She could have manipulated me and could have even gotten away with not ever telling me. I probably wouldn't have noticed. Instead, the next day she took the shoes back to the store and asked to be allowed to return them because she hadn't discussed the purchase with me. The manager of the store was so flabber-gasted that he agreed and gave her all the money back. She had repented. She could have left it there but she didn't. Instinctively my wife has always dealt out front with me. She is one of the most transparent people I know. Later that night at the dinner table she told me what she had done, com-plete with details. I can remember my feelings very well. I can remember feeling closer to her at that moment than ever before. Shortly afterward I too made the decision to be transparent with her. If she was going to level and be honest with me how could I not be the same with her? Her respect for me challenged me to treat her respectfully in return.

I am convinced that the Holy Spirit in a quiet way nudges a husband to be all that he can be for his wife. At the same time there is a deep-seated hunger in him to be looked up to and to be respected as a person, as a man, and as a man for God. The wife who learns to have respect and reverence for her husband is modeling for her husband the quality of the relationship that should exist between him and his God—a relationship that is reverent, open, and honest.

The third basic need that is present in every Christian husband is his need for his wife to be as *outwardly physically attractive for him as she can be*. The Amplified Version of the New Testament has captured what I think is a very important inference in Peter's letter. "Let not yours be the [merely] external adorning with [elaborate] interweaving and knotting of the hair, the wearing of jewelry, or changes of clothes . . ." (3:3). Some women have taken this passage to mean "don't be concerned with your outward appearance." That's not what Peter is saying. He is saying that you should be concerned with how you look but not with that only. The Apostle Paul put it this way, ". . . women should adorn themselves modestly and sensibly in seemly apparel, not with braided hair or gold or pearls or costly attire but by good deeds as befits women who profess religion" (1 Timothy 2:9–10). The most interesting word in these two passages is the word "adorn." It means to prepare or arrange oneself attractively as a bride prepares herself for the groom (Revelation 21:2). A Christian husband needs his wife to prepare herself for him as a bride does on her wedding day, with as much care and attention as is possible. Some wives have learned this and some have not. The wife who has, works at keeping herself well groomed even if the only person who will see her that day is her husband. The wife who hasn't, may fix herself up at times but when she does it's usually because she will be seen by others and not just her husband.

Thousands of Christian husbands are discouraged at this point. Because of their commitment to their wives and to Christ they have decided not to get involved in extramarital affairs even though other women are readily available. But what do they have at home? A wife who has let herself go physically to the point she is no longer attractive to him. It seems she doesn't really care. As a result, much of the motivation in the marriage is lost and a downward spiral begins. "She's not working at being attractive so I don't care. I don't care and in response she doesn't try." But he wants you to try. He needs you to "adorn" yourself for him as best you know how. Not so you can manipulate him into giving you what you want, but because he has a special need inside of him for you to demonstrate that you really care. Caring means becoming someone special for him. It is doing something about it and keeping at it. It can't hurt and it just might make a big difference.

Thus far I have discussed three basic needs every Christian husband has: the need for you to be responsive to his leadership, to respect him as a person, and to be physically attractive to him. The fourth and final basic need I would mention has to do with a woman's inner self. I like to think of it this way. *Every Christian husband needs his wife to be inwardly beautiful as a person.* Peter mentions the "hidden person of the heart with the imperishable jewel of a gentle and quiet spirit, which in God's sight is very precious" (1 Peter 3.4).

In the average woman's day there are thousands

of tensions and pressures that can figuratively shred her as a person. Her husband, her children, her job, the house, the church, the money, their schedule. The list is endless. There is usually more going on in the normal woman's life than can be managed easily. If she tends toward aggressiveness, she becomes anxious, demanding, and pushy. If her personality tends toward withdrawal, she retreats into silence, depression, and inactivity. Progressively she finds herself becoming less and less like the person she really wants to be and more and more like the person she always promised herself she would never become. As the television ad says, "what's a woman to do?" Does she become hostile and aggressive or dependent and helpless? Is there an alternative?

At this point the Christian woman has a distinct advantage. Peter suggests that just as she is to "adorn" herself physically for her husband so should she "adorn" herself for him psychologically. God desires for her to be inwardly attractive and promises the help of the Holy Spirit if she decides to take him seriously.

On one occasion I had spoken on this subject to a group of couples in a nearby church and had made a suggestion. I had suggested that women in the group who wanted to do something positive about their inward self begin by reading the thirty-first chapter of Proverbs every day for a month. After each reading they were to pick out a characteristic of the woman described in Proverbs 31 and to concentrate on the characteristic during that day. They were to ask God to point out to them where they were lacking and to show them what to do about it. The next day they were to read the chapter again and choose another characteristic. Also, I encouraged them that if they found a characteristic in the chapter that they honestly felt was already a part of their daily lives to thank God for it and to let themselves feel good about it.

A week later one of the wives came up to me after our meeting. She had faithfully completed her assignment every day for the week. During the week the verse "her children rise up and call her blessed" kept surfacing. She had become convinced that her children, rather than calling her "blessed," were instead cursing her under their breath. She heard herself shrieking and screaming at their slightest offense. Having become aware of her attitude toward her children, she asked God for the help to change. The help came from an unexpected direction. She realized that she was really very angry at her husband and that she was taking it out on the children. With this in mind she was able to confront her husband with her feelings and they were able to work their problem through. As a result, her anger and subsequent shrieking at the children diminished. That very night before she had come to our meeting her oldest teenage daughter had come up to her and told her how much she appreciated the evening meal. It had been the first time in months that the daughter had anything decent to say to her. In the short span of a week the Holy Spirit had begun to make a difference in her life and the "gentle and quiet spirit" was beginning to take form. God was alive and able to change her.

There has to be a balance between spending time on yourself outwardly and spending time on yourself inwardly. It is not a matter of either/or, it is a matter of both/and. A Christian husband, in order to be sexually attracted to his wife, needs her to be all that she can be for God, for herself, and for him. The promises are there. Why not take hold and grasp them as your own?

5

Understanding Your Wife's Sexuality

Women are different from men. They are certainly different physically and for the most part they are different emotionally. This may seem obvious, but as an observer of troubled marriages, I have found that most of the husbands who are in trouble in their marriages really neither understand nor appreciate these differences. I would even go further. I would venture to say that many husbands, even the ones with solid, stable marriages, don't fully appreciate the differences. I have to chuckle at the stereotypes and simplistic phrases that characterize many husbands' understanding of their wives' sexuality.

For example, I have noticed that men, especially Christian men, still think that women in general and their wives in particular are less sexual than they are. They can rattle off illustration after illustration of their wives' sexual refusals to support their rationale. The problem is that this just isn't true for women in general, and is becoming less true for the Christian woman. In fact, the evidence seems to indicate just the opposite. One of the most significant contributions of the Masters and Johnson research of human sexuality is that women are physiologically more sexual than men are. They are capable of greater sexual response both in terms of frequency of intercourse and degree of orgasm. Women are potentially "sexier" than men.

Then there's the stereotype that good and moral women are usually not interested in sex, that their minds are focused elsewhere. This, again, just isn't true anymore. Why? Because we are in the midst of a revolution and the revolution is affecting all women, both secular and religious. Sex is no longer thought of as a taboo by most women. They have been liberated from this burden. Even the most deeply religious women are asserting their good feelings about sex. God gave them sexual desires just like he gave their husbands, and they're beginning to expect to enjoy some of the benefits as well.

Another stereotype is that women are most satisfied if they are always the passive partners sexually and their husbands are the aggressive ones. If this were once true, it certainly isn't so today. Again, the reason is the revolution that is being lived out in this generation. There was a time, not many years past, that a wife was expected to be in the passive role. She existed as an object for his pleasure. Sex was part of her "work." Some even went so far as to define sex as the burden women had to carry because of Eve's sin.

We are in the midst of a new day, however. The dedicated "total woman" is encouraged to be all that she can be and part of that "becoming" is to be able to be sexually aggressive rather than always being sexually passive. Today's Christian woman is beginning to feel comfortable as a sexual initiator in her marriage. She no longer must appear to be shy and retiring when it comes to sex. If she wants, she is free to be all that she was meant to be.

I think this sexual revolution is good rather than bad. It's good that women are beginning to feel that they can initiate sex just like their husbands. And it's good that they are beginning to want to be satisfied sexually in the same way their husbands are satisfied, by coming to orgasm.

I have said all of this about the modern woman and her sexuality because I think the Christian husband, in order to understand his wife's sexuality, must be willing to start at the beginning. He must be willing to lay aside his assumed "knowledge-ability" and to rethink and retrain himself in the art of lovemaking.

Why? Because many husbands are grossly ignorant about sex but they're too proud to admit it. As males, most of their sex education came from less than reliable sources. Bull sessions among adolescent buddies is the most typical source. Every gang of teenage boys has its "expert." In the gang of kids I grew up with it was the guy who had gotten in trouble with the law and had been to juvenile hall. He returned from his trip to the "slammer" filled with all kinds of information. His experience earned him the mantle of leadership and he became the undisputed king of the mountain. When we started dating, he was the first to go "all the way." I was impressed with his prowess and decided that I was going to be a lover just like he was. My expertise as a lover held me in good stead for a while until I needed it most. Until I got married. It was then that I began to realize that there was more to love-making than unbuttoning and unzipping. I thought I knew it all but I didn't. There was much more to learn.

Frankly, I don't think I'm that different from most men. Even the most naïve of husbands is hesitant to admit that he is not skilled as a lover. He becomes caught in the web of *machismo,* the Spanish word that connotes sexual prowess and masculine authority. When faced with problems in his sexual relationship with his wife, the first barrier that gets in his way is his pride. It's hard for him to say, "I just don't know how to please you sexually." He'd rather blame it all on her. Many of us need help and we find it hard to ask. The first step in a husband's understanding his wife's sexuality is to admit that he's a learner.

A young couple who came to me for counseling illustrate the importance of this principle. They were Christians but their marriage was in bad shape. My initial contact with them had been a call from the wife. She had poured out her story over the phone alternating between hysteria and rationality. I agreed to see them and scheduled an appointment.

Walking into the room where they were waiting was like walking into a cold storage locker. The emotional distance between them was immense. They evidently had just finished a shrieking quarrel in the car on the way to the appointment and their silence was evidence of an armed truce. I invited them into my office. The minute they sat down the wife began to rattle off her side of the story. She had been the "faithful wife" giving him everything he wanted when he wanted it. She moaned that in return for her "sacrifice" he had gotten involved with another woman. The truth had erupted to the surface of their marriage like a volcano. She was hurt, angry, frustrated, and guilty, all at the same time. While she was erupting I watched him out of the corner of my eye. The angrier she got, the more he shut her down. At one point he was almost ready to walk out of the room.

I did my best to smooth her feathers and then turned to him for his side of the story. His rage was only slightly concealed beneath a whisper. He began to recount the "thousands of times" in their marriage that he had tried to please her but had failed. Finally out of frustration he had gotten involved with another woman. The "other woman" was as responsive to him as his wife wasn't. He was tired of being treated as the "bad guy" and was ready to throw in the towel and to chuck the whole marriage.

In the individual interviews that followed, a pattern began to emerge. He was an articulate young executive on the way up in a national conglomerate. His relationships with people were smooth and prosperous. In all areas of his life, except his marriage, he was a success. The situation was contradictory and he was quick to pick it up. He had concluded that she was at fault.

She too was a successful person. Her activities as a deaconess in their local church and a study leader in a mid-week Bible class brought her a great deal of recognition. She was admired and respected as a person. She was crushed that she wasn't able to relate as well to her husband as she was to her friends.

As successful as they were apart from each other, they were disasters in bed. Her description of him as a lover reminded me of a high school sophomore seducing his date in the back seat of his car. His technique as a lover was abominable. She was no better. Instead of telling him what she liked and majoring on the positive, she had majored on the negative to the point that he had given up. Making love to her must have been like skinnying up a tree, splinters and all.

Following a time of relationship-building I confronted them with what I thought was the first step toward putting their marriage back together. They needed to admit to themselves and to each other that in spite of their successful associations with others, they were ineffectual in their relationship with each other. Their clumsiness was most evident in bed. If their marriage was to get better they had to become "learners together." Neither knowing more than the other and neither knowing less. Both agreed to try.

But, interestingly, the husband had the most difficulty becoming a learner. Week after week slipped by with his below-the-surface unwillingness to let himself be vulnerable. Eventually I lost patience and really leveled with him. His way hadn't worked but he insisted in battling me every step of the way. I told him that it was useless for us to go on if he wasn't willing to try doing things another way. Things couldn't get worse. They just might get better.

After a long pause, he leaned back in his chair. "I've been afraid to admit that I'm wrong because that isn't been part of my vocabulary. I've clawed my way up the corporate ladder by being right, not by being wrong. Now I've got to relate to my wife differently and I find that it's not that easy." His eyes filled with tears and, turning to her, he said, "I'm sorry." They had turned the corner.

That young husband was like a Marine recruit who thinks he knows how to fire his rifle. He sees himself as quite a marksman. He keeps on shooting but can't hit the target. When his drill instructor comes around with advice he nods his head as if he is paying attention but he really isn't. When the totals are recorded he has consistently missed the target. What he needs to do is to start over at the beginning allowing himself to learn step by step. He needs to become a learner but his pride gets in the way. As long as he insists he is an expert even though the evidence indicates otherwise, he will go on repeating his errors. He must become as a little child and begin at the beginning. The husband who consistently misses his wife's sexual "target" is just like the recruit. His pride gets in the way of his admitting that he's a learner. He must begin with the first step.

Becoming a learner is the first step for most of us. The second step is almost as basic. It is the recognition that your wife is more complex than you are, both physically and emotionally. I suggested earlier that most men do not fully appreciate their wife's complexity. A husband thinks that his sexuality is relatively simple and therefore, so is his wife's. It naturally follows that the tendency is for a husband to assume his wife to be sexually aroused in the same way he is. This is so in only rare instances. Most women are aroused far differently than their husbands are.

Sexual arousal for a man tends to be determined by external stimuli, such as the presence of a sexually attractive woman. In contrast, sexual arousal

79

for a woman tends to be determined by both internal and external stimuli. Her sexuality is the complex mixture of the forces in her environment, her hormones, her perceptions of herself (that is, her self-image), and, most important of all, her perceptions of her relationship with her lover. The latter cannot be overstressed and will constitute a theme that I will return to time and time again until we've all got the principle firmly in our mind.

Assuming that a husband has done his "homework" and has nurtured the kind of relationship for his wife that will foster good sex, what is it that he needs to know in order to bring her to sexual climax?

In order for a husband to be a capable and knowledgeable lover, he needs to understand his wife's sexuality from at least two perspectives. The first is her physical sexual structure and the second is her pattern of sexual response.

Let's begin with a discussion of her basic sexual structure. A woman's physical sexual structure is the scaffolding of her sexuality. It is like the foundation of a building. As is the foundation, so are the walls of the building. If a husband wants to draw the greatest sexual response from his wife he must build that response consistently with the foundation of her sexual structure. He cannot deviate from it and still be successful. He must learn to be sexually creative within the established boundaries. Once he has come to terms with those boundaries, he is free to create and to demonstrate his craftsmanship. I'll make suggestions about that creativity in a later chapter.

What about the scaffolding, that is her physical

sexual structure? It is important that a husband understand the interrelationship between the three major components of his wife's basic sexual apparatus. These three components are first on all her bodily pleasure zones, secondly her vulva, and thirdly the clitoris.

Unlike the male, whose focus of sexual sensitivity is the glans or end of his penis, the female has many areas on her body that are potential erogenous or pleasure zones. Her breasts as well as all of the openings into her body are eligible. Her ears, her mouth, her vagina are, depending upon the individual woman, available for sexual exploration. The creative husband is not afraid to explore. His hands and mouth wander to and fro over her total body looking for those areas where she is most sexually responsive. Each day is a new day. Each experience is a new experience. And, to make it even more complicated, what is sexually pleasurable for her on one day may not be pleasurable the next. The skill a husband must develop is the skill of locating the areas that are pleasurable to his wife on that day. He then explores them in ways that are appropriate to her mood. By this I mean that there are times when a woman's pleasure zones are susceptible to firm, and aggressive, handling or touching. There are other times when firmness accomplishes the exact opposite. Rather than arousing her, the firmness or aggressiveness turns her off. At those times she is most susceptible to gentleness and softness. Very often just how a husband should proceed can be learned by asking. Or, if she finds it difficult to talk about, explore how she responds to having her breasts caressed. If the day is an "aggressive" day then she will respond to a firm and robust touch. If it is a "gentle" day she will respond accordingly. The ideal is for the two of you to be able to talk about what she needs from you so that you can vary your approach. If you're sensitive and patient eventually it should pay off. A word of warning is appropriate at this point. Routine and monotony are as deadly to a woman's sexual responsiveness as is almost anything else. Doing the same thing, the same way, time after time is deadening. Learning to vary the tempo of your touch as you explore her pleasure zones is what is most often exciting to her, always keeping in mind that you are there to pleasure her.

The second important component of a woman's sexual structure is her vulva. The vulva is the fleshy area that surrounds her vaginal opening. It is made up of the outer lips *(labia majora)* and the inner lips *(labia minora)*. The outer lips consist of two rounded puffy folds of skin which serve to protect the other parts and to preserve the mucus needed to lubricate the vaginal canal during intercourse. The inner lips are inside and parallel to the outer lips. These outward-facing folds of skin join at the top of the vulva and serve as a covering for her most important organ of sexual sensation, the clitoris. The inner lips start just beneath the clitoris and serve to outline the area called the vestibule which contains the opening of the urinary canal, and below, the external opening of the vagina. The vulva is that part of the female that is most visibly responsive to sexual stimulation. It is that part of her body that fills with blood much like the penis of a man fills when he becomes excited. At this point in our discussion the how's and why's are unimportant. What is important is that you as a husband realize it is the vulva and the clitoris (which we'll discuss shortly) that are the center of your wife's physical sexuality. It is not her vagina. Unfortunately, many husbands become preoccupied with the vagina rather than the vulva.

As an aside, there is a folk tale among the Tiv of central Nigeria that is fascinating. Long ago, according to the Tiv, every man carried his wife's vagina around with him in his shoulder bag, along with his pipe and tobacco, magical charms to protect him from witches, and whatever else constituted his daily needs. One day a very careless young warrior left his shoulder bag too close to the fire while he busied himself with work. His wife's vagina became badly scorched along with everything else in his pouch. When he returned home, his wife was so angry with him that she took her vagina away. She would no longer tolerate his carelessness. As a show of force she organized all the women of the world, and they too agreed that they would keep their vaginas with them always. Ever since that time, every vagina has been permanently attached to a woman. It no longer "belongs" to her husband.

What the Tivs have captured in folklore is a very real and central truth: the tendency for a husband to treat his wife as if her vagina really belongs to him. Why? Because the vagina is that part of her sexual anatomy that brings him the greatest sexual pleasure. Even the word connotes the emphasis. (Vagina is Latin for "sheath.") Although the vagina was designed for two purposes, to receive the erect penis in sexual intercourse and to provide a channel for the birth of a child, neither of those purposes brings her sexual excitement. The danger is for the husband to think that what is most pleasurable for him, the insertion of the penis into its "sheath," is also most pleasurable for her. This just isn't true.

Why? Because the vulva and the clitoris are the areas which hold a woman's sexual sensors, not the vagina. The vaginal canal has very few nerve endings and as a result is basically insensitive to sexual stimulation. This is why so many wives are turned off when their husbands insist on insertion too early. Once a couple have come to that point, the primary sexual stimulation and arousal for the wife is over. All that is left is orgasm and usually she's not ready. A husband needs to let his wife tell him when she wants him to "sheath his weapon." She is pleasured most by the caressing of her vulva, not by the insertion of anything into the vagina. Keep that in mind as you explore her sexual terrain.

Returning to the components of a woman's sexual structure, the last, and most important component is the clitoris. Every husband should memorize the name and indelibly etch its function onto his sexual consciousness.

The clitoris has been called the female penis and is the trigger of your wife's sexual desire. It actually corresponds to your penis in shape and development although not in size. It is located where the upper folds of the inner lips of the vulva converge. It is comprised of a glans, a shaft, and a hood. The clitoris is full of nerves and blood vessels and, like the penis, fills with blood, enlarges, and throbs when sexually stimulated.

The actual location of the glans of the clitoris is not important to your wife's sexual response because it retracts during the peak of sexual stimulation and thus precluding direct contact. Looking for the glans of the clitoris as some lovers are prone to do is not as important as stroking its shaft. Playing hide and seek with her clitoris just doesn't fit when making love.

Because the clitoris is so sensitive and is frequently the most direct means to bring a woman to orgasm, a husband needs to use caution as he explores its potential. Think of the clitoris as being as sensitive as the cornea of your eye. You would never voluntarily touch your eye directly. It would be too uncomfortable. Instead you would close your eyelid and then bring pressure to bear using your eyelid as protection. That's exactly how sensitive the clitoris is to direct touch. It's far better to bring indirect pressure to bear by means of a gentle massage of its hood. Heavy manual contact brings pain and irritation. The gentle stimulation of indirect pressure is all that is needed to bring most women to their highest sexual peak. Remember. The clitoris is the trigger, and it is the only organ in her body created strictly for pleasure.

Don't forget, however, when pleasuring your wife, the stimulation of her entire sexual apparatus is most important. Kissing, breast play, caressing, and fondling of the vulva and clitoris are what *foreplay* is all about. She is a whole person. She is not someone who has laid claim to something that once belonged to you. She is someone whose body is full of the potential of sexual excitement. She needs someone to explore that potential with her.

Enough said about your wife's sexual structure. The next step is an understanding of her pattern of sexual response.

Masters and Johnson, in their classic but highly

technical book, *Human Sexual Response,* have divided the act of human sexual intercourse into four phases. They admit that there is nothing sacred about the number except that it seemed to be a convenient division. They called these four phases (1) excitement, (2) plateau, (3) orgasm, and (4) resolution. In order for a husband to fully understand his wife's sexuality he must, either consciously or unconsciously, understand how she progresses through these four phases.

Excitement phase. A woman in the beginning stages of sexual excitement experiences an involuntary response in which tiny pores within the vagina secrete a slippery liquid lubricant and the vagina begins to get bigger. This lubrication process usually takes from ten to thirty seconds. It marks the beginning of excitement.

The next stage in the excitement phase is the engorgement of the vulva with blood, much like the penis fills with blood. The amount of area to be filled with blood is much more extensive in a woman than it is in a man. Because of this the excitement phase cannot be hurried. Physiologically a woman *cannot,* I repeat, *cannot,* speed up the time required for her to go through the excitement phase. This is why she needs her husband to take the time to prepare her. She needs him to be patient.

Next, the outer lips fill with blood and separate. At the same time the inner lips may increase two or three times in size. The inner two-thirds of your wife's vagina expands and extends so that the "sheath" is lengthened in anticipation of the insertion of the penis.

It is during the excitement phase that most of the non-genital physical reactions may begin to appear. Her nipples may become erect. Blood will sometimes rush to the surface of her skin and a "sex flush" can develop. She may perspire and experience an increase in both pulse and respiration rate. Physically tension increases within her total physical system. Her excitement builds.

Plateau phase. This phase in your wife's sexual response is when her sexual apparatus coils with tension much like a spring. Sexually she prepares for release. During the early plateau phase, more extensive changes take place in the woman than in the man. In the second half of the plateau phase the opposite occurs.

Of significant importance for a woman during the phase is the formation of the "orgasmic platform." This refers to a sack-like area that forms in the vagina when the cervix, or opening of the uterus, rises at the same time the vaginal barrel becomes larger. A pocket is formed where the semen will be deposited. At the same time the outer one-third of the vagina actually becomes smaller due to an increase in the blood supply. What is created is an ideal repository for the sperm giving them the best chance for fertilization.

Another miracle occurs at this time. The Bartholin glands, two glands located in the inner lips of the vulva, secrete a mucous substance designed to create the alkaline environment necessary for sperm to live long enough to achieve impregnation. If it were not for this secretion, the vaginal canal would be acidic and would be hostile to the sperm because the sperm thrive in an alkaline environment. God in his infinite wisdom leaves nothing to chance.

Orgasmic phase. The phenomenon of orgasm is similar for both men and women. Sexual excitement increases the supply of blood in the genital area until something has to happen. It's like a balloon about to burst. What occurs in a woman is the contraction of the muscle systems in her genital area thus forcing out some of the congested blood. The contraction of the muscles and the rushing out of fluids creates the sensation of orgasm. In a woman an orgasm causes the displacement of a great deal of blood from the congested area and provides an immense sense of relief. There are usually more contractions in the female than in the male because of the greater amount of fluid that has to be removed. This accounts for her greater orgasmic intensity.

The actual event of the orgasm itself begins with what has been described by some women as a sensation of suspension, probably caused by the contraction of the uterus. The second event is a wave of warmth that sweeps throughout her body, followed by a third event caused by the involuntary contraction of the vagina. The end result is extremely pleasurable and is usually described as a superb experience unlike anything else.

Resolution phase. In this phase your wife's sexual apparatus returns to the state it was in before it became excited. The cervix descends into the pool of semen deposited inside the vagina. The vagina contracts, and the remainder of the blood in the genital area drains back into her larger physical system. She returns to normal.

Because of the greater amount of physical involvement, a number of phenomena occur in the woman during the resolution phase that do not occur in the man. In the first place a woman is capable of more than one orgasm at a time where a man is usually not. This can happen because as long as there is congestion in the vulva there is tension and as long as there is tension there is the possibility for orgasm. Some women can experience four, five, and even six at a time.

Secondly it takes a woman longer to come down from her sexual peak than it does a man. If she has had an orgasm, ten to fifteen minutes is usually required. In a man, a minute or two is usual. Because of this physical difference, many wives need their husbands to hold them for a while in an embrace following orgasm. Some feel that this time is even better than the actual event of orgasm itself. The tendency is for the husband to roll over and go to sleep. The wife is not completely through. Orgasm for her is not the end. It only marks the beginning of the end.

The third difference in the resolution phase between a husband and a wife is of special importance. When your wife does not achieve orgasm, she is left in a physical state that for many women is extremely uncomfortable. The excitement and plateau phases have prepared her body for sexual release. The tension levels in her sexual apparatus have elevated in anticipation of the climactic event. When there is no orgasm, she is left hanging in mid-air. There is no physical release. But where does the blood go? There are no muscle contractions to force the fluids from the genitals. Her excitement then turns to irritation and rightly so. There is genuine discomfort. It is like trying to go through the day with a perpetual erection. If she feels you have hurried through your paces and have satisfied yourself without a thought of her needs, she is liable to become annoyed or even angry. The blood that would have emptied in less than fifteen minutes following orgasm, now takes as long as twelve hours to empty. The tension that would have been swept away with the blissful release of orgasm lingers on interminably. She may even feel disappointed and cheated. If she is excited time after time without achieving orgasm, what results is sexual discouragement rather than sexual excitement. You can well see why some women begin to avoid sex.

Summary. It's well to understand that when it comes to the four phases of sexual excitement, each phase is more quickly achieved and each is more quickly finished by the husband than by the wife. This is why a wife needs her husband to be patient. She needs him to take his time and to wait. The aim of experienced lovers is to go through the phases together—lovemaking is more fun when that happens.

Last of all, I would encourage each husband to think of his wife's approach to sex as she thinks of it. For her, it is an event. It is not an act. Let me use an analogy. As I write this chapter, our country has begun its Bicentennial celebration. The celebration of our nation's two hundredth birthday will last a year and a half, from January 1, 1975 to July 4, 1976. The fourth of July, 1976 will be a day marking the end of the entire celebration. The Bicentennial that culminates with fireworks and parades began with the celebration of smaller and lesser events. Something would be lost if all that was celebrated is the last day, the fourth of July. The whole country is building to the climax of the fourth of July, 1976.

So it is with your wife and lovemaking. She thinks of sex in terms of a celebration. What ends in orgasm for her begins perhaps hours, even days before. If you diminish her celebration and treat it as a five or ten minute act you are, in fact, diminishing the event itself. It may cause her to want to cancel the "fourth" itself. A husband needs to make the act of lovemaking part of the celebration of a total event. The celebration of your oneness.

6

Understanding Your Husband's Sexuality

Your husband's sexuality is deceptively simple.
Because most of his sexual apparatus is external,
much of his sexuality is similarly "out-front." His
sexual "out-frontedness" is not by chance, it's by
design. Understanding his sexuality begins right
there—with the realization that he is what he is
because God made him that way. This may seem
obvious, but it's not. It's easy for some women
to become resentful of what they consider the sexual
over-demandingness of their husbands. One wife
remarked to me that her husband was ready for sex
at all times in any place and that his sexual demands
angered her. In turn she became cold and constantly
put him off. Much to her chagrin, her shut-down
attitude toward sex produced the opposite reaction
than the one she had hoped for. Rather than being
turned off, he became even more demanding. She
withdrew and a vicious cycle of anger and resent-
ment ensued. As the three of us discussed the roots
of their sexual problems, it became apparent to me

that she was grossly ignorant of her husband's sexuality. She expected him to be able to turn on and off depending upon her slightest whim. When he wasn't able to, she became disgusted and their retaliatory cycle was begun. The healing in their marriage started with her facing the simple yet profound nature of her husband's sexuality.

To begin with, she learned that her husband was created by God to be sexually responsive to external stimuli. It's all there in the way he was designed. His genitals are on the outside and so is his sexuality. He is most vulnerable to visual and tactile movement. When she undressed in front of him at night, he would become aroused. She disgustingly attributed his arousal to lechery. But in my talking with him I found that he wasn't a "dirty old man." He was a normal, virile man who responded naturally to what he saw and what he felt. Again, the more she insisted on cuddling at night the sexier he became. She would then become resentful and retreat to the other side of their king-sized bed. He would begin his sexual pursuit and together they would run laps in the bed. Finally, after much argument she would "give in." He would crawl on and crawl off paying attention only to his physical satisfaction. She, in turn, became increasingly "frigid" and the end was a traumatized marriage.

As simple as it sounds, she needed to understand that her husband's "ready-to-go-at-any-time" attitude toward sex wasn't a result of his depravity but instead was the result of the way he was created by God. Because of man's role in the sexual reproductive cycle, he needs to be free to respond, to be free to be assertive sexually. If he becomes timid and unsure of himself, it can become difficult for him even to maintain an erection. If there's no erection, there's no sex. If there's no sex, there's no reproduction. So God created man to be a sensually exterior person, whose exteriority serves a real and useful function in the propagation of the species.

The second issue I tried to get across to her is closely tied to the first. Not only is a man's sensitivity to exterior sexual stimuli a part of the creation of God, so is his sexual vulnerability. Most young women when they first marry soon learn how physically sensitive and vulnerable a man is to having his genitals injured. Playful jousts in bed can end in pain for a man. His genitals, especially his testicles, are easily hurt, and the pain can be intense.

In the same way a man is physically vulnerable to injury, so is he vulnerable to psychological injury. If he is continually battered around sexually, by a hostile or a withholding wife, he is liable to protect himself in any way he can. Anger, criticism, and defensiveness are many times symptoms of sexual injury. Nothing feels so good to a man than having his genitals caressed both physically and psychologically. Nothing hurts as much as the opposite. Wise is the wife who tenderly and sensitively handles this part of her husband's sexuality.

This is why sex was never intended by God to be used as a weapon, by either a husband or a wife. Nowhere are we more vulnerable to each other than when we're in bed. In fact, the Apostle Paul put it this way. "Do not refuse one another except perhaps by agreement for a season, that you may devote yourselves to prayer; but then come together again, lest Satan tempt you through lack of self-control" (1 Cor. 7:5, RSV). The last part of this verse is especially relevant. Satan is clever and insightful when it comes to human sexuality. Given the opportunity, he will exploit it to the fullest.

In order for a couple to protect themselves from this temptation I would like to suggest a principle. The rule of thumb is *to say yes unless there is very good reason to say no*. This way, sex never becomes a weapon. In saying "yes" we protect our lover from the threat of sexual injury and from the "fiery darts of the devil."

There is a third suggestion I would have for wives at this point. It follows closely on an understanding of a man's vulnerability to sexual rejection. It's obvious that a wife can't always say yes at every occasion. Sometimes she can lessen the threat of rejection by learning to put it another way. She can learn to say, "Later, Dear. Not now." And then set the time. "No" to a man inevitably sounds like "never," and "never" is a terrible word.

Because a woman is put together differently sexually, it's easy for her to underestimate her husband's sexual tension. We'll discuss why he becomes sexually tense later in this chapter. It's normal for a wife to expect her husband to wait a reasonable amount of time before she says "yes." But many wives have gotten into the habit of saying "no," even when they could just as easily say "yes." They can get themselves into a position where they provoke in their husbands feelings of uselessness and undesirability. When it comes to sex, God means for us to say "yes" and not say "no." When we have to say "no" there's a better way. Say, "not now but later."

The last issue I tried to get across to this Christian wife was the one that probably helped her the most. It was that in saying "yes" she was acting in

a way that was really best for the both of them.
Having sex more often could only help, it couldn't
hurt. Why? Because, in the first place, I knew that
sexually he would wear out before she did. A wife
has that advantage over her husband. Secondly I
knew that the longer she held out, the more his
sexual tension grew. The greater his sexual tension,
the less his ability to wait for her to become aroused
and excited sexually when they did have sex. The
less he was able to wait the more frustrated she became. And the more frustrated she became, the
more she withheld sex. And on and on and on.
Someone had to do something differently.

In order to break the cycle she agreed to say
"yes" to sex as often as he wanted it. I can still see
the look of amazement that crossed his face. "You
mean you'll really let me have sex as often as I
want it?" "Yes, if you'll try your best to become
aware of my needs." He agreed and a contract was
set.

Praise God, the contract worked. The next time
I saw them, a week later, they had had sex six times.
There was an imperceptible limp to his walk as he
tried to protect his bruises (he wasn't used to the
work). He had asked for sex four times and had
gotten it six times in return. As her part of the contract she received the following. First of all, she
found that she liked sex as much, if not more, than
he did. This was their greatest surprise. Second, the
anger levels in the marriage had lessened dramatically. There were no more of those interminable
quarrels that went on for days. And third, she found
that because he was not as angry he had the motivation to become aware of her needs as a person. She
had given sex and had received love. Often that is

the case. A man will give love to get sex and a woman will give sex in order to get love. When one or the other holds out, the other will inevitably feel cheated. She gave to him what he felt he needed and the cycle was broken.

Having discussed some general suggestions regarding a husband's sexuality, we now turn to the nitty-gritty of the subject. In the last chapter I discussed the woman's sexuality from two perspectives: that of her physical sexual structure and, secondly, her pattern of sexual response. I would like to do the same with the man's sexuality.

Your Husband's Physical Sexual Structure

I have previously suggested that a woman's sexual structure constitutes the scaffolding of her sexuality. It is impossible for her to respond sexually beyond the boundaries of the scaffolding. So it is with your husband. The nature of his physical sexual structure establishes the limits of his responses.

Failure to acknowledge a man's limitations can end in problems. By saying this I mean to draw attention to what I believe to be the source of sexual frustration for many couples. It has to do with a man's "staying power." By "staying power" I mean the ability of a man to maintain an erection and to hold off ejaculation long enough for the woman to sexually catch up. I have already suggested that a man can be ready for sex and can come to sexual climax much faster than a woman. This is so because of the exteriority of his sexual plumbing. He's on the outside and, therefore, much more vulnerable to direct stimulation. She's on the inside and responds, in the main, to stimulation that is indirect.

Suppose, for example, that a couple has been married for a number of years and have a fairly stable, happy, and meaningful relationship. One problem they've not solved, however, is the problem of his "quick trigger." He can't seem to hold off his sexual climax long enough for her to become sufficiently aroused to come to climax. After years of trying, they've had little success. What's this couple to do?

A good place to begin is for the two of them to realize the sensitive nature of a man's penis. 80 to 90 percent of his sexuality is wrapped up in those muscles that hang between his legs. What happens there determines the entire course of his sexual response. If either the husband or the wife fails to realize its sensitivity, no matter how good their intentions are and no matter how hard he tries, he's not going to be able to wait.

Why? Because the penis is a muscle, and muscles are lacking in brains. True, there are neurological links to the brain itself, but as a muscle, much of the physical forces that govern sexual arousal and ejaculation are involuntary. The penis is controlled, in the main, by involuntary nervous system reflexes. This is the same part of the nervous system that controls responses such as eye-blinks and sneezing. If someone throws something at your eye, you automatically blink. If dust blows in your face, this neurological system causes you to sneeze and clean out your respiratory system. Just try not to sneeze when you really need to. You can't. So it is with the penis. When it's stimulated, it becomes aroused.

The pattern of arousal for the penis involves some

very unique and marvelous phenomena. It is made up of three parts: the glans, the shaft, and the base. These three parts consist of three cylinders, wrapped in a tough resilient, expandable sheet of skin. The inner most cylinder, the *corpus spongiosum,* contains the urethra, which conducts both the urine and the semen. The glans is at the end or tip of the corpus spongiosum. The glans of the penis is the most sensitive and erotically responsive part of the male genital. This is the part of his sexual apparatus that he loves to have stroked most of all. At its base, the corpus spongiosum ends in a bulb-like arrangement of very strong muscles which are of critical importance in the ejaculation of the semen as we'll see later. The remaining cylinders, the *corpora cavernosa,* are designed for a specific task, erection. The *corpora cavernosa* (the "caverns") are marvelously engineered compartments surrounded by a network of specialized blood vessels. When the penis is soft and in an unaroused state (i.e., flaccid) these compartments are collapsed and the blood in the penis flows quietly and freely through. With the appearance of a sexually arousing message from the brain, again involuntarily, the penis stirs into action. The blood vessels in the penis widen and blood rushes in. The compartments that were once collapsed suddenly fill to overflowing. At the same time, special valves in the penile veins are closed by reflex action thus trapping the blood in the compartments. The process is, in essence, a hydraulic system which uses blood as its liquid.

What is of special importance in the erection process is the understanding that sexual arousal in your husband involves an involuntary hydraulic system that engages in the presence of sexual stimuli.

Once the system has been engaged it becomes possible for him to maintain a state of sexual excitement for long periods of time, if he learns how. The key is to stay away from direct pressure on the glans of the penis and to stay away from friction on the shaft of the penis. Remembering that the glans of the penis is the most sexually sensitive part of a man's anatomy, if a wife wishes to help her husband keep from ejaculating too soon, she needs to learn to "play without pressure."

The next most sensitive part of a man's sexual anatomy is the scrotum, a sack-like pocket of skin that carries the testicles. The testicle, or testes, is shaped much like the female ovary. It's usually an inch and a half by an inch by one-half inch in size. It is comprised of a mass of long tubes in which the sperm is produced. Once they have been produced in the testes, the sperm move to another system of tubes in the scrotum called the epididymis. While in the epididymis, the sperm go through a ripening process that may take from two to six weeks. When the sperm are ripe they travel from the epididymis via the vas deferens through the inside of the pelvis to the seminal vesicles, a journey of more than eighteen inches. The seminal vesicles are large pouches, one on each side of the base of the penis. They act as a reservoir for the sperm and, when full, provide the man with a reminder of the need for sexual relief. Sexual tension in your husband often is tied to the overabundance of sperm in the seminal vesicles. When the reservoir is empty the pressure is relieved. Wise is the wife who keeps this in mind. When his reservoirs of sperm are low, he is liable to have greater "staying power." It's to your advantage to keep him "empty."

Once the sperm are in the seminal vesicles, they are joined by a lubricating substance, the semen, that helps them do their next job, swimming. This lubricating substance is manufactured in the prostate gland, a more or less walnut shaped organ at the base of the bladder. The prostate, in addition to manufacturing the semen, contains muscles for forcing the semen into the urethra at the climax stage of sexual excitement. At the time of sexual climax, the openings from the seminal vesicles are enlarged, and the openings of the prostate into the urethra are also enlarged, and about a teaspoon of semen is discharged along with the sperm into and through the penis.

There is obviously more that could be said about your husband's physical sexual structure, but I don't want this to become physiology. What a wife needs to know in order to understand her husband's sexuality are a few, basic facts. She needs to know what it takes to get him aroused and excited; she needs to understand the sensitivity of his penis to touch and pressure; and she needs to understand the manufacturing and storage capacity of the sperm and semen so as to appreciate his need to empty the reservoir fairly regularly. What you do with what you know is up to you.

Understanding Your Husband's Pattern of Sexual Response

Following the outline I established in the previous chapter, next is a discussion of your husband's pattern of sexual arousal.

Excitement phase. During the excitement phase in sexual intercourse, two basic phenomenon occur. First of all there is the phenomenon of erection. This usually takes from three to ten seconds and once the penis is erect, your husband is "ready to go." The second phenomenon is the thickening of the skin of the scrotum thus forcing the testicles up closer to the body cavity, perhaps as a means of protection. All of this happens quite rapidly and involuntarily. The excitement builds and your husband will begin to communicate a "need to hurry." The importance of understanding your husband's "need to hurry" and your "need to take your time" is the most important concept with regard to the excitement phase. A man and a woman are typically different at this point and a successful sex life can hinge on an appreciation and a negotiation of each other's differences.

Plateau phase. During this phase the circumference of the penis increases even more (especially the glans) and the testes enlarge. What occurs in your husband at this point has been likened to forcing air into a balloon. Once the balloon is full, the next step is to "pop." That's what it feels like to a man at this stage. He's like a balloon ready to burst. Often, intermixed with his anticipation of sexual climax is a kind of dread, a dread that he will "pop" before you do, and the realization that there's little that he can do about it.

This dilemma on the part of your husband has been identified by Masters and Johnson as "ejaculatory inevitability," a term used to describe what happens to a man at the end of the plateau phase and just before orgasm. There is a point in your husband's sexual arousal when he can do little to keep himself from ejaculating. Learning where that point is is much like learning to ident. y the topmost point of a ride on a roller coaster. Once the car has brought you to that point there's no turning back. There's nothing left to do but to hold on. We'll not go into technical details as to what happens except simply to point out that it does happen. The skill for a man of learning to wait for his wife in lovemaking is the skill of learning to identify this point of "ejaculatory inevitability." Most often what pushes a man beyond that point is the continued pressure on the glans and shaft of the penis. If he is trying to "hold on" but is afraid he can't, he should pause, relax, and try to back the car down the track before it goes over the top. Often just a few seconds' pause, or the verbal acknowledgment that he's at that point is enough. What helps most is the lessening of the pressure and the friction on the penis itself. After some practice it is possible for a man to come closer and closer to the top of the hill before actually going over. If he waits long enough, you're likely to come rushing along in your sexual car and, if you're lucky, the two of you will go over the top together. Usually at that point he'll have to hurry to catch up.

Orgasmic phase. Orgasm is similar in both sexes except it seems to be more intense in the female. When the blood in the sexual organs has filled every possible space that can be filled, a point is reached at which the surrounding muscles are caused to contact and spasm thus forcing some of the blood out of the pelvic area as well as the seminal fluid out the end of the penis.

The first event in your husband's orgasm involves the vas deferens, the seminal vesicles, and the prostate. Muscle contraction moves the sperm and the seminal fluid to the urethra. About three seconds later, the powerful muscles at the base of the penis begin to contract thus forcing the semen and the sperm through the urethra and out the end of the penis in spurts. Most of the sensation of orgasm in the male is located in the penis.

Resolution phase. Once orgasm has occurred, the compartments in the penis that were once filled with blood quickly empty. How long it takes for them to empty usually depends upon the length of the plateau phase. Erection diminishes, the testes decrease in size, and begin to descend to their pre-excitement condition. Once the congestion has diminished, your husband is relaxed and usually ready for sleep.

Again, it's at this point where the differences between a man and a woman can be sources of irritation. Because there is less blood to empty from the genitals in the man than in the woman, it's much easier for him to relax and return to normal. For him, it's over. For her, there's more. Many times the woman wants to be held and enjoy the after-glow. The skill of negotiating these differences through is what communication in marriage is all about. Each has mutually exclusive needs. How you learn to bridge those differences is what is most important. If either of you is feeling cheated, tell the other. It can't hurt and it might just help.

I'm sure that most of what I've discussed in this chapter is familiar to most women. However I would be quick to point out the difference between knowing and doing. It's one thing to understand with your head how and why your husband does the things he does. It's quite another thing to accept him the way he is and to change your behavior accordingly. Although it may not seem like it at times, a wife really does control her husband's sexual responses. She can make him feel good about it or she can make him feel bad. I've got a hunch that the woman described in the thirty-first chapter of the Book of Proverbs in the Old Testament had learned her lessons well. "She is far more precious than rubies," and "her husband rises up and calls her blessed." What has your husband said about you lately?

7

Free to Enjoy Your Sexuality

One of the greatest verses in the entire New Testament is found in the Gospel of John. Jesus was speaking to his disciples, many of whom were struggling with the overbearing nature of Pharisaical legalism. He said, "So if the Son makes you free, you will be free indeed" (John 8:36, RSV). What a statement! "Free, indeed." That's exciting. It's something we all need to grasp and hold near to our bosoms, especially when it comes to our sexuality.

In Jesus' time his followers were criticized because they had thrown off the shackles of legalism and had taken on a new kind of freedom, a freedom bounded only by love. Many times I have wished that we Christians could feel genuinely free when it comes to our sexuality. That we could experience a new kind of freedom bounded only by our love. What a difference it would make in our marriages. In fact, it's my deep conviction that genuinely liberated Christians will have the best and sexiest marriage around if they really take hold of the freedom Jesus gives. In the spirit of that freedom I make the following suggestions.

Free to Plan

The way many couples approach sex, especially husbands, really amazes me. Sex is usually a "let's do it now" kind of phenomenon. For many of us it tends to become a "here and now" event. Somehow, I think this dampens the ability of some lovers to respond. What I'm suggesting is that it is possible for sex to be a planned-for event without killing its spirit. By this I mean, some couples need to return to a courting kind of behavior as a prelude to their sexual relationship. Many of us, before we were married, spent much time and money in planning our strategy of courtship. All of that planning and it usually ended with a kiss on the doorstep. But then we got married and the need to stop at the doorstep was gone. We could go all the way to the bedroom. The problem for many of us now is that the only courting we do begins and ends in the bedroom. Sex under these circumstances becomes a one-room affair.

Where do you begin? Why not plan a special date on a special day that ends in a special place? A week-end away. A motel room. Somewhere different. There's something good and, in a sense romantic, about planning for a special time together. What's most important is that you both find a time and a place to get in touch with your special feelings for each other. I have found in my own marriage that we regularly need these special times, and they take on even greater importance when I and not my wife plan them. My willingness to do this seems to have a reaffirming effect upon my wife. Those "special" times help us feel genuinely important to each other.

Free to Be Alone Together

Children are great but they certainly do get in the way of a healthy sex life. Again, I'm amazed how little time couples really spend alone together during their average week. It's no wonder they begin to drift apart. Privacy is a must when it comes to growing a healthy sexual relationship.

If you haven't trained your children to knock on your bedroom door before entering, you should. Maybe the problem is that you don't knock on their door before you go into their room. If you don't, you should. Everyone needs a sense of privacy in order to feel good about themselves. This is especially true for the married couple. In order for them to maintain their oneness, they need time to be alone.

If your children are too young or untrainable (I don't think that's ever true—only parents are untrainable) then put a lock on your door and use it. What's important to remember is that you need to have time alone together. Fight for a time to be alone. Good things happen when you are.

Free to Lead, Free to Follow

I've already mentioned this in an earlier chapter but it's worth repeating. Nowhere in God's creation does it say that the husband is always to be the aggressor and the wife passive. It's true, that Scripture teaches submissiveness, but I don't think this is meant to rule out both partners being free to initiate sex.

Let me make a comment at this point that I think is well worth noting. It has to do with what I have observed as the growing passivity among men, especially Christian men. Years ago when I first began my study in the field of psychology, whenever sex in marriage was discussed, it was discussed from the point of view of the male. For example, I can remember lectures and illustrations about the "frigid wife" but can't remember lectures about the sexually dysfunctional husband. About the only masculine dysfunction we studied was impotence, and that only briefly. As a result, I began my professional counseling career with a bias. It was a bias that anticipated men to be functional and women to be dysfunctional when it came to sex. Much to my surprise, my first patients didn't fit my bias. Men were sexually dysfunctional as well. In fact, when I began in 1966 I was treating patients for sexual dysfunction almost proportionately between the sexes.

In the last few years, however, an interesting phenomenon is occurring. There seems to be a new, or at least new to me, problem—the "disinterested husband." This is the man who has fallen into the pattern of always expecting his wife to initiate sex. When he's not interested, he has the headaches, he's tired, etc. Whatever the causes, it's my opinion that this problem is on the increase. My armchair observations are that the problem is growing in proportion to the rise of the liberated spirit among women. Some men, in order for them to feel good about their sexuality must always be in the dominant role, always and only in the lead. When their wives begin to feel good about their sexuality the result is a threatened masculine ego.

What do you do if this seems to fit your marriage? My suggestion is for the two of you to seek sound, Christian marriage counseling. If caught before the problem is too far along, the prospects for solving the problem are high. Whatever you do, do something now, before it becomes worse.

Free to Pleasure and Be Pleasured

The concept of pleasuring is an exciting one. It has to do with allowing yourself the freedom to enjoy the physical part of your being. You were made by God to be a whole person. Part of your created wholeness is your body and its ability to be a giant receptor of pleasurable sensations. There's hardly a centimeter of area on your entire body that's not covered with sensors. Pleasuring takes this into account and takes advantage of the opportunities.

Let me quickly point out, however, that pleasuring in its fullest sense is more than a prelude to sexual intercourse. Pleasuring is that part of non-verbal communication in which each lover attempts through touching and caressing to talk with his or her hands. A husband gently brushing his wife's hair can be a form of pleasuring. Giving one another a massage using body lotion from the top of the head to the tip of the toes is another form of pleasuring. Soaping each other down in the shower or tub is another example. What is important is that each of you communicate to the other the warmth and tenderness you feel at the time.

In their book, the *Treatment of Sexual Dysfunction,* Hartman and Fithian have discussed what I believe to be a very important principle when it comes to pleasuring.

> In our culture great premium seems to be placed on speed of all kinds—in working, social situations, recreation, even including lovemaking and intercourse. Slowing couples down to warm, sensual expression of feelings and establishment of a sensual dimension, of a personality and a relationship, are basic to success in sexual therapy. If it feels good, take time to enjoy it (p. 144).

"If it feels good, take time to enjoy it." This is the essence of pleasuring. Going slow. Taking your time to touch, caress, and fondle one another. Giving yourself permission both to pleasure and to be pleasured, two sides of the same coin. When was the last time you communicated your love to your spouse in this non-verbal way? Why not give it a try? It just might bring a new dimension to your marriage.

Free to Talk

I think most of us are embarrassed to share with our lover what it is that we're feeling. Because of our embarrassment we miss out on much of the pleasure of lovemaking. This suggestion has to do with communication verbally of what it is we are feeling.

Sometimes we are verbally inhibited because we have been taught all of our lives that to talk about sex is dirty. When we make the transition into married life we tend to take this conditioning with us. Words of endearment, tenderness, and all of the sounds of pleasure are locked deep inside us lest "someone hear." So what! Let them hear. It's far better, in my opinion, for our pleasuring to be heard, even by our children, than for those around us to live in a situation in which our love is kept from them and made to be something shameful and dirty. It's not. Therefore, why live our lives as if it were?

This is not to say that we shouldn't live our love-lives in good taste and with modesty. However, modesty doesn't infer inhibition. I frankly don't think that hearing laughter coming from the bedroom will hurt our children. What would hurt them would be the open and exhibitionist demonstration of our sexuality. The line between the two may be fine, but the principle is still true. Be open with each other about your love feelings.

As an aside to this suggestion about talking to each other is the observation that many times in our lovemaking we become focused upon what doesn't feel good rather than what does. The rule when it comes to this is to accentuate the positive and forget the negative. For example, if your husband is too rough and aggressive when it comes to loving you, rather than telling him what a lousy lover he is, show him what feels good. Demonstrate for him how you would like to be touched. Don't tell him what's wrong. Show him what's right. There's a big difference between the two.

One way to do this is through the use of what is called the "non-demand" position. This technique involves the husband sitting on the bed with his back against the head of the bed. The wife sits in front of him, between his legs, her back against his chest. Both are in the nude. In this position he has access to the front of her body from the shoulders to the knees. She then takes his hands in hers placing her hand on the back of his. She shows him where and how she wants to be touched and caressed. As she moves his hands over her body she tries to tell him how it feels. Such kinds of communication can be revolutionary to a marriage. The important lesson is to focus on what feels good rather than always being critical and focusing upon the negative.

Free to Be Creative

There is something alive about couples who have a creative love life. By creative, I mean they are free to do and enjoy what feels good to them. Whether it's oral-genital sex or some new and revolutionary position, what makes it right is that it feels good to them.

Let me quickly say, right out front, that I think oral sex is okay if it is agreeable to both partners. What makes it wrong is when it is offensive to either of the partners. In Scripture it says that the marriage bed is "undefiled" (Hebrews 13:4). Sexual practices change from culture to culture and it is this influence that makes one practice right or wrong. Again, the rule of thumb would be to never do anything that would offend the other. But if both of you agree, then, in my opinion, you're free.

I think this freedom can also be exercised when it comes to sexual positions. We'll not go into an elaborate discussion of the various positions in sexual intercourse except to say that there is more than the traditional husband-superior-position. There are books both in the bookstores and at the doctors' offices that are helpful and informative. Find one, read it, and practice doing something different.

Most of all, however, creativity involves the freedom to play and be spontaneous. Sex was meant by God to be a pleasurable experience or he wouldn't have attached pleasure to it. It's a pleasure that's meant to be fun rather than work. I'm afraid that too many couples take their lovemaking too seriously. They leave their sense of humor behind rather than taking it to bed with them. Nowhere is your sense of humor more appropriate than in bed. What I'm really talking about is an attitude, one that sets your body free to run and play, to laugh and to squeal, much like a little child. Be creative. Be spontaneous. Sex can be fun.

Free to Be Patient

I include this suggestion simply for the purpose of reminding you of the need to be understanding and accepting of where each of you is at this time in your marriage. We live in a world that has idealized the sensuous man and the sensuous woman. The idealization has removed the area of sexuality for most of us from the possible to the impossible. We tend to compare ourselves and our spouses to what we think are the normal sex lives of others around us. In so doing, we can become critical, and easily discouraged.

The ideal sexual relationship is not as the magazines or movies would have it be. The ideal is what you, as a couple, are able to be for each other in the here and now. Be patient with each other. Maybe your wife is shy and more inhibited than you wish, or maybe your husband finds it difficult to be as tender and loving as you wish. What's important is that each of you make a commitment to the other to try to become more what the other needs, without the fear of criticism, but in the spirit of acceptance and patience.

Free to Be You. Free to Be Me.

Although this title has been used elsewhere as the title of a book dealing with the sexual identity of children, I think it says very well what I would like to say to end this chapter. We are all special people, created in the likeness of God and redeemed by his Son. When I think of the freedom we have because of Jesus, it touches me to the deepest part of my soul. You are good. You are God's. And you belong to each other. Go ahead and enjoy your coupleness. Being "one-flesh" is okay.

Most of all, I would encourage each of you to think in terms of tasting all that God meant for you to enjoy as a special part of his creation. Nowhere is his creation more enjoyable than in the one flesh relationship of our marriage. When each of us is all that we were meant to be then we are truly free, indeed.

8

When There Are Problems

You'll note that the title of this last chapter has been deliberately chosen. I've said *when* and not "if." The choice of words is important. Having sexual problems in marriage is normal. It's impossible for two normal healthy human beings to go completely through a lifetime together without there being some sort of adjustment in this area. I must admit that I've had individuals come up to me after I've spoken about married sexuality and that person usually brags about their never having problems in their sex life. But I've also noticed something else too. Usually only the satisfied partner speaks up. Many times the silent partner has repressed his or her feelings about the subject to the point that the other parner hasn't really heard what the other is saying.

Remember, I've spoken about lovemaking as a whole relationship only part of which is sex. I'm not saying that there are no good marriages. I am saying there are no perfect marriages. They are not perfect because we are not perfect.

This last chapter is dedicated to those of us who are in the midst of struggling through our relationship. The advice is given as a matter of information rather than as a form of prescription. As you will see, I strongly encourage couples with persistent sexual problems to seek professional help before the problems deepen and become irreparable.

What to Do If There Has Been an Affair

If modern statistics are to be believed, then the problem of sex outside of marriage is on the rise. The numbers usually range from 30 percent of women to 50 percent of men who have had sex with someone else since they have been married. What the numbers are for the Christian community isn't known, but I'm sure that they would be higher than most would think. I've said this only to point out that there is a problem.

What should you do if you are the one who is having an affair?

In the first place, I would be the last person in the world who would dismiss the problem as being a simple one. Often, if you're in this situation, you are romantically attached to the other person. You've got yourself into a double bind. You're in love with two people at the same time and that's not supposed to happen. You know in the pit of your gut that you're going to hurt someone and you don't want to face the problem head-on.

What should you do? I think the best place to start is to tell God how you really feel. Admit your predicament to him, and ask for his wisdom. After all, he's the same Lord that forgave a woman caught in the very act of adultery and sent her on her way a free person (John chapter eight). God knows your heart and so you might as well level with him.

Next, take your time. The tendency at these times is to act impulsively and to later realize that you've made the wrong decision. What I usually try to make happen when I'm working with a couple who is facing this dilemma is to get the two of them to set aside six to eight weeks of time for work and reflection before either of them make a decision about the marriage. We all need time to think and to rationally decide about our futures.

Then I usually ask the partner who is having the affair to stop seeing the other person for as long as I can get them to do it, for as long as a month if I can get it. Why? Because it's impossible for you to think straight when you're being torn apart emotionally. The only way to set yourself straight is to give yourself time and freedom to think. When you have time to reflect on your marriage just maybe you'll be able to see the time, the emotion, the commitment you've got invested in that relationship.

Last of all, I would encourage you to seriously list your options, noting both advantages and disadvantages. What will your decision do to others, including your mate, your children, and your relationship to God? Don't forget that last relationship. I've worked with scores of people who have made decisions without taking God into account and have lived to pay the price. My friend, it's just not worth it if you're a Christian.

What should you do if you're the one who has had an affair and it's over?

The biggest problem here, according to my experience, is who do you tell and how much. I have found two rules of thumb to be useful.

The first rule is that nothing should be said unless your feelings about it are affecting your relationship with your spouse in the here and now. If you're feeling guilty about it then tell God. He's the one whose forgiveness is needed. Blurting out the truth in order to expunge yourself from guilt often hurts more than it helps.

If for some reason you can't free yourself of the guilt and you are convinced it's affecting your relationship today, then find someone you can trust and talk it over. Really level with that person and let him or her know how you feel. There is a genuine sense in which confession is good for the soul. Share the truth about your affair with your spouse if and only if you have thoroughly discussed it with your confidant and only when you can confidently trust God to make good come from it in your marriage. This is the principle of "edification" as Paul discusses it in Ephesians chapter four. Truth can be good only when it is spoken in love.

The next problem has to do with the offended partner. What should you do if your spouse has had an affair?

Again, I am the last person in the world to brush this problem aside as being a simple one. I have been through too many sessions of grief with a husband or wife who is hurting in the core of their being to treat this casually.

If you're in this predicament I would first of all encourage you to find someone you can talk to whom you can trust, someone who will not sermonize you into denying your feelings.

Then I would encourage you to admit your hurt and anger to yourself, to your confidant, and to God. You have a reason to be hurt. You have a reason to be angry, very angry. The tendency for most of us is to underestimate how angry we really are. Later on it sneaks up behind us and pops out at the worst times, when it hurts rather than helps our marriage.

One of the people you're probably most angry with is yourself. Maybe you feel stupid for letting yourself be deceived. Maybe you blame yourself for letting it happen. If the truth were known you probably did have something to do with the reasons for it happening. It's too easy at these times to go to extremes. That is to blame yourself completely or to deny that you were to blame in any way. A better word than blame is the word responsibility. When these kinds of things happen in our marriage we both usually are responsible in some way. The healing cannot start until you have gotten the issue of responsibility sorted out in your mind.

Last of all, we come to forgiveness. Forgiveness at these times is easy to say but it's hard to do. Memorizing verses of Scripture usually doesn't help over the long haul. Frankly, I've found that forgiveness usually happens only after the spouse who has been offended feels their hurt and pain has been understood by someone, preferably the offending spouse. Sometimes that someone is God. At other times it is a counselor or pastor. However, the best person is the husband or wife. Try to let them know how you are hurting without becoming vindictive in the process. Place the emphasis upon "I am hurting" rather than upon "you hurt me." Say what you have to say once and let it go. Don't hit yourself over the head and don't hit your spouse either. Say how do you feel and then let it go.

The Sexually Disinterested Spouse

I've touched upon this problem in earlier chapters and therefore won't labor the point much more.

What I would like to emphasize is the fact that this is a real and growing problem in modern marriage. Very often the roots of the problem go back to how the passive partner feels about him or herself, that is, the self image. I have experienced most sexually disinterested people as having fairly low opinions of themselves. Many times they have defended themselves against this by becoming dominant or aggressive. When their partner begins to feel good either spiritually or personally, they begin to withdraw and become passive.

The answer is to seek the advice of a trusted professional who will treat the problem fairly and openly. Most of all, if you're the "disinterested spouse," do something about it yourself rather than waiting for your partner to act. If you insist upon waiting you're only adding to the problem.

Problems of Sexual Arousal

As I write this part of the chapter I am acutely aware that there is a danger to treat the problems of sexual dysfunction lightly and in a cursory manner. I certainly don't want that to be inferred by either what I say or don't say. I fully recognize the complexity of the issues under discussion and include the following sections for purposes of education rather than therapy. Hopefully, those who are struggling with these issues in their marriage will take heart and seek professional help and relief.

Men and women who have difficulty getting sexually aroused have much in common. Words such as "impotence" and "frigidity" have been bantered about with very little understanding on the part of the average reader. Problems in the area of sexual arousal have to do with the inability or retarded ability of the genitals to respond to sexual stimuli. Because the penis or the vulva fails to trap the blood necessary for congestion, there is no erection in the man and there is a lack of lubrication and swelling in the woman. There are no simple answers as to why this happens. Often the treatment requires intense counseling and encouragement. But it is treatable. The roots of the problems go often to messages in the brain that inhibit our sexuality from being freely expressed. Where those roots go, is a question best answered by those trained to help. If either you or your spouse find it difficult to become sexually aroused then it's best you talk to your medical doctor and ask him to refer you to someone trained to handle these kinds of problems.

Problems of Sexual Orgasm

This category of problems include such problems as the non-orgasmic female, as well as premature and retarded ejaculation in the male. In this situation, the genials do become sexually aroused. There is swelling and lubrication in the female and erection in the male. So that part of the problem is settled.

What is left has to do with the inability to manage the orgasm effectively. Most often the problems lie in the relationship and the inability of the couple to negotiate and communicate their feelings about sex and about other issues in their marriage. Fortunately, of the problems having to do with sexual dysfunction, the "cure-rate" for these kinds of problems is the best. You simply have to find someone who knows what they're doing and set about the business of solving the problem.

Again, as in the previous instance, consultation with your medical doctor is the first step followed with referral to a professional who has been trained to treat these kind of problems.

Conclusion

If I have tried to say anything in this book it is that good, healthy, sex between a husband and a wife is based in the quality of their relationship. If that relationship is in trouble usually their sex life will be also. When there are problems between you sexually, look first at the relationship. Evaluate your patterns of communication. Check out your priorities. If, after you have surveyed the state of your marriage and there are still problems that seem to be beyond your ability to solve, then be willing to do something about it.

Don't wait until the problems are so immense that only a miracle will help. Have the sense and the courage to find someone to talk to who can either help or refer you to someone who can. We live in a day and age when the best of us need help sometimes. The truly wise among us have come to grips with this and have done something about it.

Not all of us need professional counseling but more of us could use it than actually seek it out. If you find yourself in this position, take a deep breath and do what's best for your marriage, even though it may hurt your pride.

READING LIST

Christian: Celebrate Your Sexuality, Dwight Harvey Small (Old Tappan, New Jersey: Fleming H. Revell Company, 1974).

Concordia Sex Education Series (St. Louis, Missouri: Concordia Publishing House).

God, Sex and You, M. O. Vincent (Philadelphia: J. B. Lippincott Company, 1971).

Love, Sex, and Being Human, Paul Bohannon (Garden City, New York: Doubleday and Co., Inc., 1970).

Sexual Happiness in Marriage, Herbert J. Miles (Grand Rapids: Zondervan Publishing House, 1967).

Understanding the Female Orgasm, Seymour Fisher (New York, New York: Bantam Books, 1973).